Studies in Women Writers in English

Studies in Women Writers in English

VOLUME–II

Edited by

MOHIT K. RAY
RAMA KUNDU

ATLANTIC
PUBLISHERS & DISTRIBUTORS

Published by
ATLANTIC
PUBLISHERS & DISTRIBUTORS
B-2, Vishal Enclave, Opp. Rajouri Garden,
New Delhi-110027
Phones : 25413460, 25429987, 25466842

Sales Office
7/22, Ansari Road, Darya Ganj,
New Delhi-110002
Phones : 23273880, 23275880, 23280451
Fax : 91-11-23285873
web : www.atlanticbooks.com
e-mail : info@atlanticbooks.com

ISBN 81-269-0337-6 (Vol. II)
ISBN 81-269-0338-4 (Set)

Printed in India
at Nice Printing Press, Delhi

GENERAL PREFACE

The series is about women writers in English across centuries and spaces; the subject is the major women writers in England and outside, who happen to be women, whom we read and will continue to read, because they fascinate us by raising questions, opening perspectives, challenging, illuminating and explaining life. It seems indeed striking when we consider the fact that so many of the great writers of modern times have been women. Particularly since the eighteenth century, women's contribution to the field of literature has been indispensable. In the subsequent history of literature women have emerged as both central and female.

To set out some of the parameters of the anthology's goal: it attempts to represent a variety of methodological approaches to literary texts instead of a particular methodology, or focusing on a specific theme. The idea is to attempt as much comprehensiveness as possible. Without being exclusive it attempts to include studies on minority or marginal/subaltern literature as well as "mainstream" subjects, and to represent a broad spectrum of perspectives, by bringing together as many authors and views and areas as possible.

Indeed, "feminism" itself stands for no monolithic, unified or singularly definable concept; rather the multiplicity of approaches and assumptions inside the movement can be stunning as they conflict and compete with each other. The present series will take into account the diversity not only within feminism, but also within women's writings in general. Again, in spite of the multipleness of feminism, a generally shared agreement among feminist critics has been that gender leaves its traces in literary texts and literary history. In the context of the increasingly interdisciplinary nature of literary studies today, newer insights have been harnessed to probe and bring out these unique 'traces' which have enriched women's writings in the past and the present.

We hope the book will provide some sense of the scope, the variety, and the development of women's literature in English in the recent centuries. The boundaries of the book have not been set arbitrarily but by the subject itself, which seems to have been set to cross all previously laid boundaries; while reading the earlier writers anew as women writers, from today's critical perspectives, will also prove to be an exciting experience.

Finally, lest some raise the issue whether segregating some writers from the general course of literary history just on the basis of sex is fair or not, this may be noted that great women writers teach us how everything special to a woman's life—from its most trivial to its grandest—can be claimed for literature by writers who possess what Thackeray saw in Charlotte Bronte: "the passionate honour of the woman."

The series is designed for use in courses on "Women in Literature" and at the same time addressed to many other audiences outside the university classroom, who will find it useful and enjoyable.

MOHIT K. RAY
RAMA KUNDU
Editors

PREFACE TO VOLUME TWO

English is being written and read today by more people outside England than inside. This applies no less to the women writers in English across the globe who have made their unmistakable mark in English literature[s], especially in the last century. The present volume,—the second in the new projected series of APD, *Studies in Women Writers in English*—bears evidence to this phenomenon as the critics address women writers in English in various parts of the globe rather than concentrating on canonised mainstream authors and texts, and thus mainstream writers figure only referentially, (excepting one essay comparing Christina Rossetti with Emily Dickinson) in the margin of these critical texts, as it were. Again, understandably Indian writers take over a chunk of the space. However, the essays included in this volume cover authors from America, Canada and India, and also some theoretical discourse regarding feminism and marginal literature. The authors discussed in this volume are Christina Rossetti of England, Emily Dickinson, Harper Lee, Lorraine Hansberry and Sylvia Plath of America, Margaret Atwood of Canada, and Kamala Markandya, Kamala Das, Nayantara Sahgal, Anita Desai, Githa Hariharan of India. Apart from this a wide spectrum of Indian writers have been referred to and treated in the general articles on feminist theory and practice, especially in India today, and yesterday.

Partha Pratim Dasgupta attempts a comparative study of Christina Rossetti and Emily Dickinson, the British and American women poets of the nineteenth century, with reference to their shorter poems, and brings out the connection between the necessary constrictions of their life and the nuances of their poems.

Harper Lee's *To Kill a Mocking Bird* is a familiar name to the Indian reader since it has surfaced frequently in studies of Arundhati Roy's *The God of Small Things*. T.M.J. Indra Mohan makes a brief survey of Lee's Pulitzer-winning novel of 1960 and brings out its humanitarian focus on race relationships against a South American backdrop.

Anita Singh discusses Lorraine Hansberry's *A Raisin in the Sun* (1959), the first play written by a black woman to be produced on Broadway, as a milestone in black women's drama, and a protest play addressing conventional notions of an insensitized society. Ms Singh perceptively brings out Hansberry's sympathetic examination of the economical, educational and racial concerns of a family of black Chicagoans.

Nandini Sahu finds both Sylvia Plath and Kamala Das, the American poet and her Indian counterpart, engaged in the act of using poetry as a 'therapeutic process,' a way of coming to terms with the exceptional female energy that characterises both the poets.

Rama Kundu probes Margaret Atwood's use of 'mirror' as a trope with reference to the emerging icon of the 'foremother' or 'ancestress' in *écriture feminine* across the globe today.

Santwana Haldar appreciates Kamala Markandaya's *Nectar in a Sieve* for focusing on a marginalized area of Indian life, but also contends that as a study of agrarian life in colonial India the novel seems inadequate, and not sufficiently realistic.

A.K. Awasthi relates Kamala Das's art of poetry to the Indian concept of the "Dance of Shiva,' and makes a close study of seven poems of Das to show that the imagery in the poetry of Kamala Das faithfully illustrates the dance of nature and wisdom of soul, known as the 'Dance of Shiva.'

Beulah Ranjitsingh highlights the emergence of the 'New Woman' in Nayantara Sahgal's novels. The author studies two novels of Sahgal, *Storm in Chandigarh* and *The Day in Shadow* to show how Sahgal's female protagonists go through conflict, frustration, stress and bitterness to eventually find a stable identity of their own.

Ajay Kumar Ghosh surveys the entire creative corpus of Anita Desai to bring out the novelist's preoccupation with complex human relationships, often between partners of incompatible temperament.

Mohua Ghosh examines Githa Hariharan's novel *When Dreams Travel* as a feminist text which uses the frame of an ancient tale to inscribe 'Her Story' from a modern feminist perspective. In her second essay Ms Ghosh shows how Githa Hariharan interrogates the patriarchal assumptions in the layered text of the *Arabian Nights,* and at the same time writes a self-reflexive postmodern novel by means of creative departures from the source.

Jaydeep Sarangi investigates the nature of cross-cultural tensions, conflicts, confrontations and alliances portrayed in the works of Bharati Mukherjee and Jhumpa Lahiri, and places this in the discourse of diaspora, cross-culturalism and multiculturalism.

Smriti Singh uses a wide range of reference to probe the extent to which the image of the 'New Woman' has been emerging in the English novel by Indian woman writers, and how do they tackle the problem of constricting past values on the way to self-fulfilment.

Shyam S. Agarwalla analyses the variegated shades of feminist approaches, and contests that much of Indian feminist outbursts against "roles of mythological females" are based on the logocentric studies of India. He also questions the so-called "feminist obsession with the one-dimensional study of

Sita." While appreciating some of these writers for their "authentic voice," Agarwalla concludes that Indian feminism is marked by "contradiction and overdetermination," a view to which many people may not agree.

T.M.J. Indra Mohan makes a brief historical survey of feminist thought and movement for social change in the last century, and claims that feminist thought will eventually emerge as basically a humanistic thought.

The essays of the volume will be found interesting as well as useful by students, teachers and scholars and will also be enjoyed by the general readers.

We thank all the contributors for their perceptive studies.

We are particularly thankful to Dr K.R. Gupta, Chairman, Atlantic Publishers and Distributors, New Delhi, for the confidence evinced in us, and for seeing the book through the press.

MOHIT K. RAY
RAMA KUNDU
Editors

CONTENTS

1

LIFE AND ART: A COMPARATIVE STUDY OF CHRISTINA ROSSETTI AND EMILY DICKINSON

PARTHA PRATIM DASGUPTA

I

Ever since the neologistic coinage of the term 'Gynesis' (Jardine 261) and the conscious emergence of the 'Gynocritics' (Showalter 248), the trajectory and psychodynamics of feminism and feministic criticism has been enriched to a never-before height of culmination. Showalter's condemnation of Terry Eagleton and Jonathan Culler for their lukewarm approaches to feminism might have emerged from an individualistic perspective study. But the way in which she discerns a "treachery in both the male erasure and embrace of feminism" (Kauffman 2) and subsequently warns all feminist critics to beware of a 'male theory' seems rather unnecessary and slightly far-fetched. It is not always necessary that the male attitude towards feminism or feminist criticism is essentially phallogocentric or pornoglossial in a camouflaged form. As Toril Moi proclaims: "I see no reason why a man should not proclaim himself a feminist" (Moi 180), though critics like Elaine Showalter would inevitably regard such male support of feminism as 'Cross-dressing.'

This paper attempts a comparative study and perspective criticism between a British poet and an American poet of the mid-nineteenth century: Christina Rossetti (1830-94) and Emily Dickinson (1830-86) by taking into consideration their shorter poems.

II

The socio-attitudinal milieu on both sides of the Atlantic ocean during the mid-nineteenth century was more male-chauvinistic than it is today. Woman, 'the Angel of the House' to quote the title of a poem by Coventry Patmore via a reference by Virginia Woolf in her essay 'Professions for Women,' is a symbol of dependence (perhaps a malapropism for 'drudgery') beauty and carnality. She can be allowed to spend some time in the innocent hobby or pastime of composing rhymes on flowers and children as long as it did not hamper the normal household responsibilities or made something like a 'demand' upon the Head of the House's purse. Ruskin (1819-1900), the celebrated social reformer and critic of the nineteenth century made the following observation about the conception of 'Home' to a female in the Victorian age:

> It (the 'Home') is the place of Peace; the shelter, not only from all injury, but from all terror, doubt and division [...] a vestal temple, a temple of the hearth watched over by Household Gods, before whose faces none may come but those whom they can receive with love [...]. (Ruskin 100)

Such theorizations should be regarded as conceited attempts to mislead and subsequently chain the women to the enslavement of domesticity without their own knowledge. The 'limited range' of Jane Austen and the Bronte sisters in the realm of novels and Elizabeth Barrett Browning and Fanny Fern (Sara Willis Parton) in the sphere of poetry has time and again been highlighted by the male critics suffering from imperfect reading position, a theory propagated by Anne Cranny-Francis. When Donald Barlow Stauffer in his *A Short History of American Poetry* (1974) presented us with a critical account of seventeenth century poetry, he preferred to spend a few of his valuable lines for Anne Brandstreet (1612-72) as the only poet belonging to the fair sex who somehow deserved a mentioning. Jean Gould in her book *American Woman Poets* humorously pointed out that when Edna St. Vincent Millay's poem 'Renascence' was published in 1912, such established and knowledgeable poets as Wilter Bynner and Arthur Davison

Ficke, probably without bothering to read the poem itself, strongly argued that a sweet little "thing" of twenty was incapable of probing into the depth and vision of the Renaissance; only male poets of their age and calibre were capable of handling such a complex theme. Vincent Millay retorted to their allegations by emphatically saying that she "simply would not be a male!"

It was only John Stuart Mill (1806-73) who understood some of the discrepancies mented upon the female and chose to discuss it impersonally and unbiasedly in his essay entitled 'The Subjection of Women' (1889):

> The social subordination of women stands out as an isolated fact in modern social institutions, a single relic of an old world of thought and practice exploded in everything else [...]. (Mill 21)

III

Three important themes that manifest themselves in the poetry of both Christina Rossetti and Emily Dickinson are (i) Loneliness and alienation, often caused by death, (ii) Love, seen from the perspective of a woman and (iii) the dearth of alternatives in all spheres of life available to a woman. In order to trace the reason behind the conscious or subconscious choice of these similar themes, a psychobiographical probing into some aspects of the lives of these two poets seems needful. The lives that the two poets lived and the poetry they wrote have the mist of an enigma hovering over them that has not dispersed till date, even after a century-long critical debate.

Loneliness was not Christina Rossetti's choice, it was something that was imposed upon her by providence. Actually she began as an energetic girl, full of vitality and aspiring like her brothers for fame as a writer. Her love for outdoor life and sociability received its first jolt when she started developing a number of ailments during her adolescence. These ailments have often been termed by critics as "mysterious" (Gilbert & Gubar 893) as the actual nature and symptoms of these diseases were never divulged by her. As Drabble observes, "Ill-health (possibly strategic when young, but later severe) ended her attempts to work as a governess, and confined her to a quiet life" (Drabble 844). These ailments certainly cast their dark shadows upon her psyche. Her attempts towards finding economic liberation by working as a governess at the age of twenty-five proved so strenuous and demanding upon her frail health and hypersensitive nature that she wrote to her brother William: "I am rejoiced to feel that my health does really unfit me for miscellaneous governessing en permanence" (Gilbert & Gubar 893).

Actually, from the age of twenty-five itself, Christina Rossetti's physical ailments, had incarcerated her into a private world of premature retirement from active life coupled with seclusion. Her brief and abortive attempts of living an active social life in the form of working at St Mary Magdalen Home for Fallen Women on Highgate Hill or with Florence Nightingale's expedition of nurses to Scutari were no doubt modern as per the standards of the times but they proved as fluctuating as her frail health. Her father's serious illness that left him bedridden for almost ten years till his death in 1854, the mysterious suicide of her sister-in-law Elizabeth Siddal, wife of Dante Gabriel Rossetti had cast a pall of gloom permanently upon her sensibility. Christina Rossetti had never got on well with her sister-in-laws, whether it be Elizabeth Siddal or Lucy Brown, the wife of her younger brother William Michael Rossetti. Christina Rossetti doted upon both her brothers almost like Dorothy Wordsworth who, according to Bateson, was the Lucy of her brother's celebrated Lucy poems. Whether it was sexual jealousy at her brother's new found conjugal-happiness or a feeling of insecurity caused by her feeling of being ousted by the two new ladies whose youth and beauty were constant reminders to her that she was past her prime rather too prematurely that roused in Christina Rossetti a feeling of rivalry with her sister-in-law, we do not know for certain. Thyroid malfunctioning coupled with serious bouts of Graves' disease made Christina Rossetti go so alarmingly disfigured that she felt ashamed of making public appearances. A feeling of weakness that never seemed to desert her made her feel her room and her bed as her safest retreat. Her younger brother William Michael Rossetti was very disturbed due to the growing "tension" (Drabble 894) between his sister and his wife and when the problem grew unsurmountable, he had to part with his sister and subsequently his mother and his aunts and find a separate lodging for them, much to his dismay. After the death of her mother and two aunts, Christina Rossetti lived harrowingly alone till the loneliness of her life was finally relieved by cancer in 1894.

During the last phase of her life, Christina Rossetti's wild and eccentric behaviour was the cause of perpetual disturbance to her neighbours. A week before her death, she started screaming at the top of her voice for long hours during the evenings and continued this to the last day of her life. If the screaming was the result of some pain, it was more mental than corporal; it should be seen more as hysterical outbursts than as manifestation of a temporarily disturbed state of mind. The psychologists interpret 'hysteria' as "a psychoneurosis in which repressed complexes become split off or dissociated from personality, forming independent units, partially or completely unrecognised by consciousness, giving rise to hypnoidal states (amnesia, somnambulisms), and manifested by various physical symptoms, such as ties, paralysis, blindness, deafness, etc., general features being an extreme degree of emotional instability and an intense craving for affection: an outbreak of wild emotionalism" (Kirkpatrick 620). It was probably Christina Rossetti's loneliness, her alienation and her suppressed libido that found their outlets through such behavioural patterns.

For Emily Dickinson, loneliness was more invoked than imposed. From the very beginning of her poetic career, Emily Dickinson felt seclusion to be one of the essential preconditions for her creativity. Her parents provided her with almost no mental and emotional support that she needed while growing up due to their inability to read her mind. They never understood her. Simply to talk to them on matters above the mundane was difficult for the hypersensitive girl. The parents executed their formal responsibilities rather proudly and pronouncedly without ever thinking it needful to fathom her emotional and intellectual necessities; they neither shared nor encouraged Emily Dickinson's aesthetic pangs for creativity. Their evident failure to be role models before their silently demanding daughter is evident in the writings of Emily Dickinson:

> My mother does not care for thought [...]. My father seems to me often the oldest and oddest sort of foreigner. Sometimes I say something and he stares in a curious sort of bewilderment, though I speak a thought quite as old as his daughter [...]. (Johnson and Ward, eds. 29)

The pain of being unloved, misjudged and abandoned therefore started taking a permanent shape in the psychic pattern of Emily Dickinson from the very formative stage of her life. The result was inevitable. She eschewed society and started turning inwards. Gradually her loneliness started being less claustrophobic to her and changed into the very source of her sustenance. She strived to know the colours, contours and the conditions of loneliness. With none to fulfil her emotional and intellectual demands, Emily Dickinson withdrew to her room in the second floor of the house and sometimes wrote but mostly conversed to herself.

Two forces that attempted to grind Emily Dickinson into the self-same Amherst womanhood who were forced to perform the twin functions of being brainless bodies and child-minting machines were (i) her domineering and headstrong father and (ii) the theological 'opium' of the Congregational Church against which she had to combat tooth and nail for the sake of her intellectual survival. This resulted in the gradual hardening of her sensibilities both for her biological father and the 'Father of the skies.' Alan Shucard, in his article entitled 'Emily Dickinson and the Two Modes of Romanticism,' very rightly suggests that much of Emily Dickinson's behavioural politics and poetry were a reaction against her father. It can be well said that the protest was against the 'Father of the skies' too. Emily Dickinson's Calvinist father Edward Dickinson was a successful lawyer of Amherst, Massachusetts and belonged to a world both distant from and detested by his daughter. His chidings, far from bringing any supposed betterment upon Emily Dickinson, made her a rebel. Even when Emily Dickinson had been a mature adult, the father tried to mastermind and even censor her reading habits, dress codes and small attitudinal traits like receiving guests. This over-insinuation of the father made Emily Dickinson lose all her reverence for the man. Thus loneliness was Emily Dickinson's way of finding an escape from the drudgery inflicted upon her by her parents, particularly by her father.

It is needful to point out the attitudinal difference between Emily Dickinson and Christina Rossetti about religion. Though Emily Dickinson grew up in an orthodox Christian family, she never suffered from any exaggerated trait of devotion. Her mind was rational not religious. The Evangelical revival at Amherst in 1844 never touched Emily Dickinson as such and left her rather indifferent. Mabel Loomis Todd, who brought out the first published volume of Emily Dickinson's poems in 1886, four years after the poet's death, referred to an incident narrated by one of Emily Dickinson's ex-classmate. Mary Lyon, the principal of Emily Dickinson's school once addressed the students of the would-be poet's class. Her religious fervour quickened by the newly enkindled Evangelical revival, she asked all students who wanted to be true Christians to "rise." Everyone apart from Emily Dickinson stood up. Through her gesture Emily Dickinson proved at that tender age that she detested participating in any buffoonish and melodramatic religious show.

In a letter to Higginson in 1848, Emily Dickinson wrote about the religious mindset of her parents and how her attitude differed largely from them:

> They are religious—except me—and address an Eclipse, every morning—whom they call their 'Father' [...]. I have perfect confidence in God & his promises & yet I know not why, I feel that the world holds a predominant place in my affections. (Johnson and Ward, eds. 47)

In another letter to Higginson, Emily Dickinson deglamorises and humanizes Christ:

> To be human is more than to be divine, for when Christ was divine, he was uncontented till he has been human. (Johnson and Ward, eds. 56)

Devoid of its theological reverence, religion emerged merely as a book of metaphors to Emily Dickinson that actually reflected, to quote a line from one of her poems, the "flecked Human Nature."

What brings these two poets of two different continents even closer is that both of them had been losers in love and had known the pangs of languishment. Cupid first struck Christina Rossetti when she was a blooming maiden of eighteen. In this case her beau was James Collinson, a painter as well as a poet and more importantly, one of the active members of the Pre-Raphaelite Brotherhood. After they were well in their courtship stage, it was religion that came in between the lovers and tolled the knell to their dreams of marital bliss. On 1850 James Collinson, Christina Rossetti's fiancé, converted himself to Roman Catholicism. The Rossetti family were devoted and orthodox High Anglicans and greatly influenced by the Tractarian Movement. Christina Rossetti's two brothers Dante Gabriel Rossetti and William Michael Rossetti had some flexibility in their attitude towards religion, but Christina Rossetti, who lacked exposure like her two brothers and had grown up within the overtly orthodox and stern Anglicanism of her home, could not rise above the limitations imposed by religion. After much mental oscillation, Christina Rossetti decided to sacrifice her love at the altar of religion.

Probably Christina Rossetti repented her decision later but there was no way in which she could rectify her stilted relationship with Collinson. To pacify her inner torments caused by a feeling of guilt for having wronged a gentleman, for superficial reasons, Christina Rossetti started feeding herself voraciously with Italian and English religious poetry. But the grief within her found no relief; it solidified into such an unhealing psychic wound that Christina Rossetti dangled halfway in between the principle of religion-ordained renunciation and her lust for life that accounts for the rich artistic tension in her poetry. Thus it can be said that whereas Emily Dickinson showed the power of withholding the stranglehold of religion upon both her emotional and intellectual sensibilities, Christina Rossetti could not rise above the limitations ordained by religion.

Christina Rossetti's younger brother William Michael Rossetti said that another love affair that eventually led to his sister's suffering was with Charles Bagot Cayley. Encouraged by her, Cayley summoned the courage to propose to her in 1866 but was refused. This led to the suffering of the proposer but the one proposed was believed to have suffered even more. This incident may be interpreted in two ways: (i) probably Christina Rossetti no longer believed in the formality of institutionalized marriage; (ii) instrumental as she had been in breaking her first engagement with Collinson, probably Christina Rossetti felt herself being morally questionable to him if she accepted the hand of Cayley. Probably she had not quite forgotten her first love.

Lona Mosk Packer, one of the biographers of the poet, has brought in a third candidature in her insightful observation of Christina Rossetti's inner life. She seems to suggest that consciously or unconsciously, Christina Rossetti was desperately in love with a married family friend named William Bell Scott, much like Emily Dickinson. As in the case of Reverend Charles Wadsworth who reciprocated Emily Dickinson's love rather lukewarmly, remaining always within the constrains imposed upon him by marriage which, most obviously, he had no intention of sacrificing. William Bell Scott also acted like Wadsworth while reciprocating Christina Rossetti's love for him. Christina Rossetti's younger brother William Michael observed that much of the pain of his sister's poems resulted directly from her emotional turbulence and broken relationships in love. There can certainly be an exaggeration in this observation as rightly pointed out by the critics. But the fact that Christina Rossetti never married and resigned herself to a life of seclusion may be studied as an attempt on her part to weed off these painful memories that had almost embossed themselves permanently upon her attitude and understanding of life.

Though Emily Dickinson attempted in her own way to shroud her emotional life in an aura of mystery, critics focus upon her letters to Reverend Charles Wadsworth, a handsome, charming and married person who reciprocated her love through silent acceptance while remaining within his constraints. Having met him during her stay in Philadelphia in 1855 when she was a girl of 25, Dickinson maintained regular correspondence with him and was visited by him twice. In all her letters to Reverend Charles Wadsworth, she addresses him as 'Master' and prefers to compare herself to a 'culprit' (as psychologically she is in the thick of an extramarital affair), to a wounded bird (*i.e.*, helpless; at the will and whim of a hunter and desperately needing some care), to a child-like "Daisy" (*i.e.*, in her full bloom and longing to bask in the love of an admirer) and a "smaller life" (*i.e.*, willing to merge into the bigger life and forsake her own identity). Critics have rightly found in her letters to Reverend Charles Wadsworth an eroticism often frankly alluded to or represented in a codified form.

It is also believed that Dickinson shared a tender relationship with Samuel Bowels, the then editor of *Springfield Republican* whom she "sent and addressed" (Drabble 271) many poems with, but mostly without, any intention of getting them published in his magazine. Probably it was her unrequited love for both these married men, with different intensity levels though, that convinced her not to enter into the prisonhouse of marital relationships.

The above discussion goes on to prove that these two contemporary poets on both sides of the Atlantic had passed through similar experiences that could have attributed to some of the similarities of perspectives and preoccupations as reflected in their poetry.

IV

In spite of their minor attitudinal differences, Christina Rossetti and Emily Dickinson come close to each other particularly in the realms of three kinds of poetry:

1. Mortuary Verse

The first common theme that found articulation in the poems of both Christina Rossetti and Emily Dickinson was the theme of death. Rossetti's handling of the theme of death is uniquely individualistic. Her poems about death have neither the morbidity of the Jacobean dramatists' representation of death, nor do they come near the Graveyard Poetry of the Pre-Romantics in their attempts to philosophise death. So Christina Rossetti's poems about death should better be called mortuary verse rather than memento mori verse. Sometimes

Rossetti's attitude towards death is soft and sentimental; at other times mystical or mysteriously sensuous and at times even heavy with existential pessimism.

In her poem 'Song' the poet or the poetic persona ruminates upon death. She forbids her 'dearest' to sing sad songs for her after her death or make an elaborate and exaggerated ritual by strewing roses on her grave. The speaker would prefer the beloved to metamorphose himself into the 'green grass' that would be wet 'with shower and dewdrops.' Death therefore emerges as that interjunctory phase that seems to increase the tactile sensations rather than lessening it. The beloved, by transforming himself into grass, would ooze the moisture of nature in the form of rain or dewdrop into the transfixed state of the lady's existence attained through death. The reader is made to believe that in her tranced or drugged state inflicted by death, the lady would welcome such ardent and symbolic touches of her beloved but she would be past the power of reciprocation. Nature therefore takes up the functional position of enjoining the world of the dead and the world of the living in this surrealistic and mystical way. The image of the shower and the dewdrops infiltrating into the world of the dead as if to fructify it has a high sensuousness that is almost Keatsian in its intensity. The image has a dimension that is erotically suggestive too.

Death seems to have transported the speaker into a state past flux where everything seems frozen into a transfixedness though probably, it is far from being either idealized or harrowing as the theologies ascertain. But the poetic persona also apprehends that death would eventually transport her into a world of oblivion where her nostalgic memories of love will be robbed off from her.

The balanced attitude of the poet to this interrelations among love, death and memory is very striking because in the hand of a lesser artist such themes have often been reduced to a chaos of confused and unrestrained sentimentality. Nostalgia admixed with sorrow provides the poem with rarefied artistry that the simple diction reiterates throughout.

Rossetti's sonnet 'After Death' may be regarded as the lineal progression of the emotions developed in the previously discussed poem. Here the speaker or the poetic persona imagines herself as dead. But death, far from lulling her into sleep had quickened her perceptive powers. At the opening of the poem, the chiarascuro technique is brought into focus. With light through the 'hald drawn' curtains reflecting upon the 'swept' floor in angular strides, the lady lay on her death-bed, apparently lifeless but somehow more receptive to the atmosphere of mourning that seemed to have reached a point of saturation. 'Rushes, rosemary and may' hurled one upon another on her death-bed are all emblems of spring; they denote that the sad demise of the lady had occurred untimely, at the spring of her life and in stark contrast to the fresh lease of life, manifest in the world of nature.

The lady's silent and unreceptive lover now leans over her bed. Through her intuitiveness the lady could well read her beloved's mind which went on murmuring words of longing and repentance, realize his inward urge to clasp her hand and look into her face, something he had not done in her lifetime. The lady's longings for love had gone unrequited during her life. Her languishing heart is now mortified by the fact that even after her death, she is not actually loved but largely pitied:

> He did not love me living; but once dead
> He pitied me; [...]. (896)

The poem ends somewhat ambiguously where the lady seems to find some recompense by the fact that she might have passed into a world devoid of warmth but her loved one is still throbbing and pulsating with life. Probably the speaker seems to suggest that the essence of her life had passed into her beloved and only intensified his vigour through this strange transmigration that had enabled her to pour all her warmth and love into him.

'Dead before Death,' another mortuary sonnet by Christina Rossetti, opens with the chill of lifelessness running down the spine of the reader. The apprehension of imminent death has 'stiffened' the smile of the poetic persona and killed the lustre of her eyes. The lady is conscious of the external and corporal changes brought upon her by death but the spirit remains unchanged. Even the large share of experiences of life does not succeed in changing one's basic attitude. Much good is promised during the penultimate phase of life but little of it is delivered by destiny in reality. One only grows hollow both physically and emotionally; the process of decay actually starts even before death begins decomposing the body.

> Grown hard and stubborn in the ancient mould,
> Grown rigid in the sham of lifelong lies:
> We hoped for better things as years would rise,
> But it is over as a tale once told. (897)

The body and the mind, far from being a source of joy, becomes a burden during the old age. The existential pessimism of the poem is reiterated by the word 'lost' that has been used five times, though not in a series. It reminds one of the brooding pessimism at the end of Shakespeare's *King Lear* where Lear howls at the face of fortune: "Never, never, never, never, never" (Act-V, Sc-III, 1-308).

The image of the 'fallen blossom' that 'no fruit bore' is striking as it points to a state of emotional as well as physical barrenness, an inability to procreate in spite of the best of intentions due to abstinence from physical relationship or the fear of social censure or some other repressed apprehension. The temporarily ajar door that is called life only allures but never yields. The door is ultimately shut off by death that puts a stoppage to the suffering from 'chime to chime.' Death therefore liberates one from the slow smouldering in the eternal bonfire of life. The image of death as revealed in this poem has two dimensions which are diametrically opposed to each other. Death is both the enslaver and the liberator of mankind, with or without their being conscious of it.

The physical as well as the psychic process of death is one of the focal themes of Emily Dickinson's poetry too. Some of her poems show her absorption, almost an over-preoccupation with death. Death is both omnipotent and omnipresent as it, like the sun, infiltrates into any place it wishes to pay a visit. In poem no. 465 the poet or the poetic persona transports us into the world of stillness and the silence of death. The silence is so overwhelming and nerve-wrecking that even the buzz of a fly is audible loud and clear. The sudden stillness that had descended as if from the thin air seemed only a temporary state that could apprehend the fearful emergence of a storm. The storm seems to be heaving a sigh to mourn the death of the poetic persona. Somehow a camaraderie between the natural world and the human world seems to have emerged. Contrary to this emotive bondage the eyes of the mourners were dry after shedding many a genuine or superficial tears; they were breathing (not sighing) more out of discomfort than genuine pain. The speaker had a faint suspicion that these people had assembled only for the sake of signing her off after covering her coffin with some formal mementos.

Seeking a keepsake among the pile of mementos spread like debris, the speaker's eyes alighted upon a fly. The blue body of the fly seemed to cast a hypnotic spell upon the persona assumed by the poet. The fly seemed to constitute a bridge between the dead and the translucent light where her departed soul would merge. The speaker felt her senses pass into this light as gradually her sight and senses began to bid this world adieu. While commenting on the image of the fly, Allen Tate observed that the fly comes to stand in its sinister and abundant life for the privation of life, the body of the young woman on bed. Callow and Reilly regard the fly as "a symbol of doubt over the fate of her soul, but certainly a reminder that her body would soon become food for insects" (Callow and Reilly 4). Both these two critical opinions prefer to see the fly in a negative connotation. Yet a deeper study of the image convinces the reader that the speaker seems to be cast into a region of accidental hypnotism by the fly; she does not look at the fly with eyes of repulsion. For her the fly seems to be the agent or the messenger that would transport her to the infinitely better world of death by tolling the knell upon the sequence of meaninglessness of life.

Emily Dickinson's celebrated poem no. 712 begins with the oft-quoted lines:

> Because I could not stop for Death—
> He kindly stopped for me—
> The Carriage held but just Ourselves—
> And Immortality. (877)

The usual host-guest, giver-seeker interrelationship that human beings and death share between themselves seem to have been reversed here. With the silent articulation of reverence due to a celebrity. Death waits upon the speaker with utmost politeness and does the speaker proud by sharing the carriage with her *en route* immortality. The mutual ride, punctuated by patience, seemed so spontaneous and unobtrusive to the speaker that both 'labour' and 'leisure,' two apparatus used exclusively for measuring the drudgery called life, had lost all significance in this journey.

The carriage window opened up the vistas of still or animated life like fields overflowing with grains silhouetted by the last crimson rays of the setting sun or the gleeful school children. Nature suddenly seemed to beam with beauty and the zeal of being, now that Death is the speaker's silent, solitary, understanding and uncomplaining companion. As they went past the sunset, leaving behind the finitude of the small world, silence being their only language, dewdrops, falling in profusion, gradually soaked into the fine silk net with which the lady covered her shoulders. Some Freudian critiques have found in the lady's sudden realization that her dress is transparent a nightmare of sexual humiliation. All that can be said about this observation is that it is certainly one way of interpreting the poem but not the only way.

The speaker soon saw the sensate world giving place to a dilapidated edifice that resembled a grave. Callow and Reilly interpret the carriage as the 'hearse' and the dwelling as a 'tomb' (Callow and Reilly 4). Marshall Walker believes that the poem is "written from the point of view of someone who had been dead for centuries [...]. The tone of acceptance implies faith in 'Immortality,' her companion on journey; the memory of mild surprise adds pathos" (Walker 119).

The speaker does not tell us where this surrealistic sojourn eventually ended. We are led to believe that the physical journey ultimately turned psychic. The poem ends with the speaker-poet's realization that many centuries had passed apace since Death, the noblest and the politest of presences that she ever chanced to meet, took her along in a journey beyond the horizons of the world and enabled her to have a feeling if not a glimpse of eternity. We are also made to believe that such journeys never really end; it is a continuing process reaching beyond the grave, a compendium of many a life and the ongoing process of transcendentalism that makes one realize the ultimate blissful heights that Death can transport one to.

In poem no. 1445 of Emily Dickinson, Death emerges as the 'supple suitor' who, through his silence and patience, finally wins over everyone he chooses to cast his love-lorn glances at. The eternal love affair between Death and Life begins first by the former's wooing the later through gentle, polite and patient persuasions. Gradually this 'dim approach' catches momentum and reaches the predicted culmination when Life succumbs to Death. His love's labour won rather easily, Death carries Life to unpredicted facets of experience where, in the new light of self-realization, the left-behind kith and kin—once so very dear, have no significance at all. Therefore the poem fuses eros and the thanatos by showing life and death entangled in an eternal love-relationship.

Death, as we find in these three poems of Emily Dickinson, is not the conventionally harrowing or terrible figure as represented in theology or ancient literature. Rather Death is a solicitous suitor and an agent of seduction. Some critics have found an element of 'morbidity' in Emily Dickinson regarding the way in which she provides the interrelationship between love and death an aura of courtship. Psychoanalysts have read in Dickinson's presentation of Death the images of a father, a lover and a narcissist which they think is also true about the poems on the theme of death by Sylvia Plath. Emily Dickinson's poems on the theme of death puts forth no theological debate concerning the essential opposition between the body and the soul. Her individualistic rendering makes death as original and unconventional as her poems. Dickinson's attitude towards death reminds one of a few lines from one of George Eliot's letters:

> For death seems to me now a close, real experience, like the approach of autumn or winter, and I am glad to find that advancing life brings this power of imagining the nearness of death I never had till of late years. (Haight 121)

Indeed, for Emily Dickinson, death seemed another state of existence. Through her apocalyptic imagination charged with a psychological insight, Dickinson almost concretizes something that is, in its essence, indescribable.

Thus we find that both Christina Rossetti and Emily Dickinson shared an ambivalent attitude towards death in spite of their variegated attitudinal differences.

2. Love Poems

Love, sometimes requited but mostly unrequited uncoupled with the pangs of languishment both mental and physical, is a favourite poetic theme that Christina Rossetti shared with Emily Dickinson. Confronting the enormity of loneliness can be suicidal at the initial stage but for a responsible, respectable female standing with her head high, it is also a way of being transported to a fascinating world where everything seems symbolic and codified. Love, imagined if not real, therefore adds some meaning to an otherwise vacant life.

Christina Rossetti's poem 'The Birthday,' one of the brightest and happiest of poems that she ever wrote, arrests the ecstatic mood of a love-lorn lady. The simple incident of the beloved's return takes the speaker to such heights of joy that she feels her heart singing like a bird. She even feels herself like the bough of an apple tree bent down by the weight of innumerable ripe and juicy fruits which probably symbolizes fructification and the new birth of love. A rainbow seems to appear in the horizon of her heart and the speaker realizes:

> My heart is gladder than all these
>   Because my love is come to me. (899)

The poem ends with the speaker's emphatic instruction that a high raised platform, hung with silk and ornamentally decorated, should be constructed for them immediately, probably to serve the purpose of a marital bed.

Emily Dickinson's poems nos. 209, 211 and 249 are quite close to Rossetti's poem 'The Birthday' in revealing more or less similar experiences of love. In Emily Dickinson's poem no. 209, the speaker leaves behind all her bashfulness and expresses her ardent desire to be with her beloved in the most adverse of conditions, without the slightest complaint:

With thee, in the Desert—
With thee in the thirst—
With thee in the Tamarind Wood—
Leopard breathes—at last! (860)

The words 'thirst' and 'leopard breathes' coming along with the expression 'at last' seems to suggest the joyful apprehension of consummation after long spells of physical and emotional drought.

Poem no. 211 of Emily Dickinson expresses the ardent passion of love in a symbolic way. The advancement of a lover is shown in conscious parallelism with the stealthy movements of a bee that lowers into the bosom of a Jasmine and drinks deep the nectar accumulated therein. Two 'lips,' unaccustomed as they are, will take time in knowing each other and once they had done so, the embalming 'nectar' would drug them into 'dizzy raptures' and prepare them for the 'aching joys' of physical consummation. The lines of the poem ooze a warmth that is almost palpable.

Dickinson's poem no. 249 shows us how the wild and windy nights increases the languishment swelling in the heart of the lady-love:

Wild Nights—Wild Nights!
Were I with thee
Wild Nights should be
Our luxury! (860)

The winds would be futile if it is unable to hasten the union of the lovers. The lady feels her heart had been reduced to the helpless position of a ship in a turbulent sea that is without any compass and charts to follow a right course. The lady feels that it would have been much more cherishable if the lover had been the sea where the lady would like to row the ship of her soul. The use of the navigation imagery is reminiscent of Shakespeare's sonnet no. 116 and John Donne's metaphysical conceits, particularly in his poem 'The Good Morrow.'

Christina Rossetti's poem 'A Triad' is another love poem that treats the theme in a complex manner. The title actually refers to a musical chord formed by three nodes. In an impressionistic manner, the poem describes the love-lives of three female singers who gave solo performances of love songs but mostly sang together. The first singer seemed to be the very embodiment of the love-song she sang—her 'crimson lips' and 'aglow bosom' denote that she had been able to strike a fine balance between the themes of her song and their culmination in her own life.

But the two other singers had not been so fortunate regarding their love-lives. The second singer, in spite of her best attempts, was not able to fully hide her sense of alienation and lovelessness. She sang in a soft and smooth voice but it lacked the warmth of life and love; she looked like a 'tinted hyacinth' who had made herself up for a 'show.' The gaiety and festivity had failed to stimulate her though she continued with her routine performances with all professionalism but no heart.

The third singer's physical as well as mental condition appeared even more dismal. Her love had gone unreciprocated and hastened upon her soul a feeling of premature barrenness, reiterated by the image of the 'famine.' Her voice played the role that the bass part plays in music; it is therefore 'harsh and low' and has an element of discord and disjunctiveness in it.

Eventually the outcome of love in the case of all the three singers turned out to be more or less the same. The first lady who shone in the glow of love ultimately brought ignominy upon herself, probably by breaking the conventional codes of morality that mattered not to herself but to the society. Whether all these troubles and shame brought her the much coveted satisfaction is a question that goes unanswered; but the intonation of the poet leaves an element of doubt about the outcome. The second lady settled into wedded permanence if not ease and found herself in the thick of 'soulless love' (*i.e.*, sexual relationship alone where the two minds remain as alienated as ever) till she found herself change to a cunning and conniving wife. The third singer pined her way to her grave. Therefore for two of the ladies, love led to the darkness of death both real and psychic and for the third one, love proved to be a life-in-death, an eternal onward march through everlasting pain. This, in short, is the contours of love and its subsequent impact upon the lives of the three female singers and in a broader connotation all women of the world.

Poem no. 754 of Emily Dickinson is another love poem that has an element of evasiveness in it. The poet compares her life to a neglected gun that had been kept at one corner of the house and completely forgotten. One day it was accidentally picked up by the owner and whimsically carried along. Once the owner was able to understand the power and capacity of the gun, he started carrying it in every hunting expedition though it was questionable if, in reality, he developed any love for it. Its individuality minimized, the gun lay beside its master's bed and cast its languishing glances on him.

The sudden capitalization of the words 'My Master' may appear as a personal eccentricity on part of the poet but when we recall that Emily Dickinson wrote a lot of intimate letters to Reverend Charles Wadsworth where she addressed him as 'Master' throughout, the problem is resolved. Treated with utmost passivity, the gun realizes its tragic fate: it will go on killing without itself having the power to die. The tragic plight of the gun is an embodiment of the lady's own condition. She deliberately stays close to her 'Master,' longs every moment for the reciprocation of her love and yet he remains insensitive to her all through. Longing and languishment reaches an element of universality here, particularly as articulated from the perspective of a female.

To Christina Rossetti and Emily Dickinson love can therefore be an intensely emotional and hypersensitive state of mind that can be dreamt about, discussed, debated, cherished, fantasized and even intellectualized over. In spite of its evanescence, its transitoriness and its futility, the seven shades of a rainbow seem to have aptly manifested themselves in the two poets' delineation and handling of love.

3. Subaltern Poems

Another theme shared by both Christina Rossetti and Emily Dickinson is the dearth of alternatives available to the women of the nineteenth century and also to women in general even today. While reading their poems one is time and again reminded of one of Gayatri Chakraborty Spivak's observations in her celebrated article entitled 'Can the Subaltern Speak?'

> [...] the subaltern as female is even more deeply in shadow. (Williams & Chrisman 78)

In fact Christina Rossetti's poem 'A Triad,' as discussed in the previous sub-section, can be regarded as a study of the tragic plight of womanhood left with no alternatives apart from being a wife or mistress of a man for the sake of survival. Her intelligence, her capacity and even her emotions ruthlessly minimized, she is forced to live the life of a beautiful puppet, exposed to every whim of the male who prefer to be her instigator and helm the course of her life without bothering to take her opinions about it. A part of the Marriage and Divorce Act, 1857 of Great Britain can be cited to show how biased the attitude towards women during that age was. The Act said that a wife can easily be divorced for adultery but as infidelity and promiscuity were inherent qualities of the male, they cannot be divorced for the same charges.

In the poem 'A Soul,' Christina Rossetti focuses upon the essential alienation and eventual helplessness of women in the essentially hostile and male-dominated world. She invokes the archetypal image of Cleopatra standing with a venomous Egyptian snake close to her bosom during the last hours of her life. Standing all alone like an ancient statue made of white marble, her face 'pale' and cast towards the 'shadowy land' of death, she had witnessed too much of the male-centred world to have any illusions about it. Men have lusted for her body, raised their eyebrows to find a woman rule a country and eventually pulled her down from the throne because their egoes could not bear the rule of a woman. In spite of her intelligence and her capacity, she was left with no alternative but to conform to the given norms of a male-ordained world. Her pride and her power still manifest in her gait though her soul was sore, Cleopatra stands all alone like a lighthouse in the storm-tossed sea. With an essential fellow-feeling, the poet hails the eternal rebel lurking in every woman like the spirit of Cleopatra:

> Indomitable in her feebleness,
> Her face and will athirst against the light. (896)

One Cleopatra might have been forced to find a release from the shackles of a malevolent, male-oriented world through suicide but the Cleopatras to come would rise like the Phoenix from her ashes and spread their luminous wings all over the globe.

Poem no. 288 by Emily Dickinson is at one level a poem about the poet's ardent wish to live a private life but from another level it is also a poem about how a woman is often reduced to the position of a nonentity if her appearance or life-style does not stimulate an admiring glance from a male:

> I'm Nobody! Who are you?
> Are you—Nobody—too?
> Then there's a pair of us? (862)

A woman therefore needs to be 'beautiful' and sycophantic towards the male if she wants to climb up the social ladder and be a 'somebody.' With such absolutistic social norms made by the males, the poet would be happy enough to be a 'nobody' and suffice in this state of existence.

Seen from a broader perspective, Christina Rossetti's poem 'In an Artist's Studio' speaks about the problematics of the representation of women in the visual arts by giving the example of Dante Gabriel Rossetti's portrait paintings, particularly those in which he used his would-be wife Elizabeth Siddall and sometimes even his sister, the poet herself, as his models. The male painter fondly goes on using his colours and crayons, lost in the sensuous artistic zeal of arresting the beauty of his female models, clothed and unclothed. But they never think about what thoughts pass through the minds of the women who pose for them for hours at a stretch in most uncomfortable or disagreeable postures and gestures according to the painters' whims. And whether the portraited female herself appreciates her exposure or simply likes to be a property for posterity to ogle or leer at is a question that is never asked to the female model:

> We find her hidden just behind those screens,
> That mirror gave back all her loveliness.
> ....
> A nameless girl..............................

....

The same one meaning, neither more nor less. (915)

As a manifestation of love, respect, obligation or even pecuniary considerations, a woman is forced to pose as a model sometimes robed but mostly unrobed. At the cost of her exposure, in all the possible connotations of the term, the artist becomes famous but the woman remains as nameless as ever.

In poem no. 1072, Emily Dickinson points out the discrepancy between the idealized picture of woman and the plight of woman in reality. Women are often given an aura of divinity in theory; they are the much loved 'wife' or 'Empress' of the heart. Such conferring of titles upon women, the poet obliquely suggests, is merely a lip-service. It is another way of deception which the women fail to understand. With the sarcasm becoming of a myth-breaker and a truth-teller, Emily Dickinson points out the hypocrisy that men had used from the very beginning of creation to cunningly ensure the slavery of women:

Royal—all but the Crown! (881)

Betrothal is often the happiest moment of a woman's life but what she does not realize is that it is another step towards enslavement and servitude. The progress of women in life is summed very aptly in the cryptic but harrowing image:

Born—Bridalled—Shrouded—. (881)

The necessity of a total change in the biased attitude of the society against women is pointed out by the avid enquiry at the closing lines of the poem that rings loud and clear in our ears:

Is this—the way? (881)

Christina Rossetti highlights the miserable plight of women forsaken by their husbands in her poem entitled 'Enrica, 1865.' If a woman is abandoned by her husband it is all but natural, but if the woman does the same, it is a sheer instance of profligacy—such are the value-judgments of the world that is essentially male-oriented. In this poem Christina Rossetti speaks about a lady called Enrica Barile, an Italian lady who was abandoned by her husband. Ironically enough, the husband, after abandoning his wife, changed his name to 'Filopanti,' an Italian word meaning "all loving" and probably went away to prove the mantle of his new name elsewhere. Here Rossetti also offers us a glimpse into the conservative and conventional attitude of the English women towards life, who dream but dare not work out these dreams in real life for fear of public censure:

We Englishwomen, trim, correct,
All minted in the selfsame mold,
Warm-hearted out of semblance cold,
All-courteous out of self-respect. (917)

This self-analysis and self-evaluation can be regarded as that preparatory stage when the English women were desperately trying to rise above the restrictions imposed upon them by the society and find their own emancipation.

In the poem no. 1737, Emily Dickinson speculates the charges most likely to be labelled against her after her death. Some would say that she lived half a life due to the fact that she never married and therefore never knew the fulfilment of a wife or the affections of a mother. Others would speculate that if her sensibility be measured, she was a replica of a 'bearded man.' At such accusations hurled upon her in profusion, she would prefer to blush from her new position attained through death.

Years of fidelity *fide et amore* to the aesthetics of her artistic creativity had made her learn more of life than she could have learnt through matrimony and motherhood. She had also experienced love in her own way unlike the narrow self-seeking love of partners sharing domesticity; she had remained constant in very trying situations. But this love and constancy was not towards any person but to the Muse. At present everybody regards her as the crowned queen of poetry, but during her own lifetime, she had actually worn a crown of thorns that equates her suffering with that of Christ. In an age when a woman had almost no alternative apart from being a wife and mother, this poet had the courage to think and act otherwise.

Thus we find that women, the "oppressed and the silent minority," of the nineteenth century, to quote a phrase from

Nancy Armstrong's 'Desire and Domestic Fiction' (1987) voice their feelings and emotions, intellections and epiphanies in and through the poetry of Christina Rossetti and Emily Dickinson who, in spite of their differences, came close to each other in opening up new vistas and newer horizons that the poets-to-come can traverse and carry along to newer heights.

NOTE

All the poems of Christina Rossetti and Emily Dickinson are noted in the text with appropriate page number(s). Details of the edition is noted in Works Cited.

WORKS CITED

Callow, James T. and Reilly, Robert J. *Guide to American Literature From Emily Dickinson to the Present.* Barnes & Noble Books, 1977.

Drabble, Margaret, eds. *The Oxford Companion to English Literature.* Oxford University Press, 1998.

Gilbert Sandra M. & Gubar Susan. *The Norton Anthology of Literature by Women.* Second Edition. W.W. Norton & Company, 1996.

Haight, Gordon S., ed. *The George Eliot Letters & Selections from George Eliot's Letters.* Oxford, 1954-78 (9 Volumes) and 1985.

Jardine, Alice A. *Gynesis: Configurations of Woman and Modernity.* New York: Cornell University Press, 1985.

Johnson Thomas H. and Ward Theodara, eds. *The Letters of Emily Dickinson.* 3 Vols. Cambridge, Mass.: Harvard University Press, 1958.

Kauffman, Linda. *Gender & Theory: Dialogues on Feminist Criticism.* Basil Blackwell, 1990.

Mill, J.S. *The Subjection of Women.* London: M.I.T. Press (rep.), 1970.

Moi, Toril. *Men Against Patriarchy.* Ed. Kauffman Linda. *Gender Theory: Dialogues on Feminist Criticism.* Basil Blackwell, 1990.

Ruskin, John. *Sesame and Lilies.* New York: John, Wiley & Sons, 1885.

Showalter, Elaine. *A Literature of Their Own.* London: Virago, 1982.

Walker, Marshall. *The Literature of the United States of America.* Macmillan, 1988.

Williams, Patrick and Chrisman Laura, eds. *Colonial Discourse and Post-Colonial Theory: A Reader.* New York: Columbia UP, 1994.

2

HARPER LEE'S *TO KILL A MOCKING BIRD*: A PORTRAYAL OF HUMAN VALUES

T.M.J. INDRA MOHAN

Over half a century, the literary world has been witnessing writers in different genres focusing the racial discrimination, especially in America. Sometimes they are lopsided, on a few occasions they are balanced and we cannot fix a definite neutral or judicious writing propounding a black voice against suppression or objective portrayal of the lives of the blacks as well as whites in a social structure within the ambits of human values. But in this respect Harper Lee is different. She probes the psycho dynamics of the people from both the black and white races and how they encounter their problems when mutually affected. *To Kill a Mocking Bird,* Lee's Pulitzer Prize winning novel in 1960 illustrates the point Harper Lee was born and raised in a small town in Alabama. Her study of law and its principles helped her develop a vivid prose style. Her southern upbringing provided her with enough raw materials, which she incorporated into the novel. Her book became an instantaneous success world over, the primary reason being that the novel was the first of its kind to anticipate a beginning for black-white understanding. It is also regarded as one of the best novels of the period to portray the American South in contemporary literature.

According to R.A. Dave in the novel *To Kill a Mocking Bird* a small world assumes macrocosmic dimension and expands into immensity, holding an epic canvas against which is enacted a movingly human drama of the jostling worlds of children and adults, of innocence and experience, of kindness and cruelty, of love and hatred, of humour and path and above all of appearance and reality, all taking the reader to the root of human behaviour.

Harper Lee makes a bold attempt to bring together two dominant themes of contemporary Southern fiction—the recollection of childhood among village eccentrics and the spirit-corroding shame of the civilized white Southerner in the treatment of the Negro.

Lee's attempts to portray the social order as she witnessed in her locale find expression in graceful writing and genuinely moving and mildly humorous excursions into the transient world of childhood.

The story is set during the depression wherein we see Jeen Louise (Scout) Finch, whose widowed father, Atticus, was a civilized and a congenial lawyer in a backward town in Alabama. An older brother, Jem, and a summer visitor from Mississippi, Dili, share Scout's adventures. The narration abounds with buzzing village gossips and most especially, with the mysterious occupants of the house next door who has never been outside since his father locked him up fifteen years ago. It is through Boo Radley whose invisible presence tantalises the children, that Miss Lee builds the most effective part of her novel.

In the second half of the novel Atticus defends a Negro accused of raping a white girl. He upsets his neighbours by defending a black. Through Scout's eyes we watch the growth of resentment in the community, and then we see the trial itself, in which Atticus is inevitably defeated. The existence of caste systems in the power of the sexual taboo, has been called "the strongest taboo of the system" in the Southern part of the American society. This is well dramatised by the maneuverings during Tom Robinson's trial for allegedly raping Mayella Evell, a central episode in the novel.

Although Tom's infraction of the Blackman-white woman code is demonstrated to have been false, he is nonetheless, condemned. The caste taboo overrides empirical evidence. Atticus remarks to the Jury, "Those are twelve reasonable men in everyday life, Tom's Jury, but you saw something come between them and reason [...]. There's something in our world that makes men lose their heads, they couldn't be fair if they tried." In spite of the fact that the whole case involves so much of doubts and missing links as to the guilt of the black man, the chief witnesses for the prosecution. Tom Robinson is condemned. We learn from Atticus that the entire prosecution is based upon "The assumption, the evil assumption that all Negroes lie, that all Negroes are basically immoral beings, that all Negro men are not to be trusted around our women." The conviction of Tom bears enough evidence to the hold of caste-oriented assumptions in actual life.

As typical as its caste system is the ubiquitous system of class distinctions among the whites. Harper Lee's characters fall into four classes: Old aristocracy represented by Atticus Finch's class-conscious sister, Alexandra to the poor white train represented by Bob Ewell and his brood who have been the disgrace of Macomb's for three generations. While presenting the interaction of these three classes, Lee provides a matrix of the traditional social stratification of the American South.

The subtleties of the southern class distinctions are brought out vividly by Harper Lee in this novel in which her ultimate aim is to transform the social structure for the good of every one living not only in part of the continent but in the whole world. At the same time the novel recognizes the diversity of mankind and still the diversity is unified by a set of higher laws, which cannot be ignored. A slow change emerges in the attitude of the southern people towards their traditional past. Maycomb town people who see through the fog of the past, and who act not from tradition but from principle, which Harper Lee focuses, suggest a way for the possible salvation of the South.

The central character of the novel, Atticus Finch, is the individual who vibrates to his own iron string and he is a trustworthy companion to the community in the town. He is a typical southerner. He understands the problems of the people. He understands the difficulties of Tom Robinson though he is black. In short Finch is a graceful and simple person. He is not an idealist, but believes in the ultimate goodness of mankind. During the course of his argument in the courtroom he acknowledges his belief that "there is not a person [...]

who never told a lie, who has never done an immoral thing, and there is no men living who has never looked upon a woman without desire." Finch does not discriminate in this analogy between black or white; as a human being he looks at the fellow human beings within the ambit of good and bad nature prevalent in everyman.

In Lee's *To Kill a Mocking Bird*, she embodies the South in Maycomb and its residents. It has necessarily accept its place in natural life structure. Like Emerson's concept of the individual, Maycomb must be no longer hindered by the name of goodness, but must find out what precisely goodness is meant to be. To a thoughtful and perceptive observer, the old ways have lost their value, new ones must be found to supplant them, if on the other hand, the old ways stand up to the doubtful eye, they should by all means be preserved. True to this principle Atticus Finch has acted and he has taught his children to act. By extension, the South must do the same, preaching good, cultivating good that it possesses, and thereby it can seek a unique place in the national history.

The theme of persecution in the novel also takes us back to the ancestor, Simon Finch, who sailed across the Atlantic to escape religious persecution in England, keeps the victims off the stage, invisible while the tension between the protagonist minority and the antagonist majority shake the world of Maycomb with an ever increasing emotional and moral disturbance. All this is presented in a fascinating way with flashbacks, and the continual back thrust intensifies the unforgettableness of the narrator's experience. Maycomb is a small world. The novelist's creative mind has peopled it well. We have a cross section of humanity—men and women, young and old, good and bad, white and black. On the whole the novel presents a memorable portrait gallery. Lee's emotional and moral bias seems to put her more at ease with good people than bad. The wicked characters tend to be hazy and the good characters stand out prominently throbbing with life. Bob Ewell and his associates are paper figures. The women in the novel are better portrayed than the men with the exception of Atticus. Her best portrayals are in the characterization of children manifesting them with the possession of admirable qualities. Lee's next best creation is

Atticus, the dignified and reticent protagonist. When the entire white world seems to have lost its head, he remains sane. He is a good combination of strength and tenderness. He has a stoic resistance in the midst of opposing forces. It is in the trial scene that we see Atticus at his best, exposing the falsehood and meanness of the white world intent on destroying an innocent Negro. If Jean Scout, the daughter, keeps the wheel of the story turning, Atticus is the axle. He is noble and firm.

Though Harper Lee is not a modern, she stands to be ranked a contemporary novelist. The contemporaneity of *To Kill a Mocking Bird* is incidental, its universality essential. In a characteristic way Lee tells the story of a past age. She has an unusual intensity of imagination, which creates a world more living than the one, which we live, so very solid and easily recognizable. Lee has viewed one of the most fundamental human problems in essentially Christian terms of reference. We see emerging from the novel a definite moral pattern embodying a scale of values. It is not a work of propaganda. As we read the novel, we notice an unfailing murder arising out of the flux of experience. It is the evolution of human consciousness elaborated through the chain of events. There is a cohesion of art and morality and therein lies the success of the novelist. *To Kill a Mocking Bird* in short is a criticism of life.

REFERENCES

Harding Lemay. "Children play; Adults Betray," in *New York Herald Tribune Book Review*, July 10, 1960.

Hicks, Granville. "Three at the outset," in *Saturday Review*, Vol. XLIII, No. 30, July 23, 1960.

Fred Erisman. "The Romantic Regionalism of Harper Lee," in *Alabama Review*, Vol. XXVI, No. 2, April 1973.

3

LOOK BACK IN GENDER: LORRAINE HANSBERRY'S *A RAISIN IN THE SUN*

ANITA SINGH

As the dreamer is the author of the dreams, so, too, it is the polis or community that makes the stories it tells in its drama. The struggle to define women's proper place in the theatre has been going on for at least 2,500 years and shows no signs, as we stand on this new millennium, of being resolved.

Among the most perturbing of such theatre are those by black American Women playwrights. For them there is a complicated double consciousness in which they see the world as an American Woman and a black woman. From the beginnings of theatre by black women playwrights to the present, these women's dramas have tended to create stage worlds in which diverse voices and world-views collide, polyphony is asserted and sometimes celebrated and different signifying systems of dance, music and visual imagery are aggressively utilized.

The black, long either a subject of indifference or, at best the concern of self-conscious white writer, began to speak for himself/herself with greater force from the early twentieth century. Lorraine Hansberry's *A Raisin in the Sun* (1959) was a milestone in black women's drama. It was the first play written by a black woman to be produced on Broadway, and the first play by a black woman to win New York Drama Critics Circle Award. The play, a domestic comedy with overtones of emotion, some close to soap opera, is out of ordinary in its warm, human way with blacks whose problems, not unlike those of families everywhere looms so much larger simply because their skins were dark. Written in the political and cultural ambience of the Integrationist Movement it is a social protest play intended to persuade white people that black people are not only good at heart but sufficiently like whites in their values and cultural practices for whites to allow blacks to be their neighbours. The title of the play taken from Langston Hughes's verse:

> What happens to a dream deferred?
> Does it dry up
> Like a raisin in the sun?
> Or fester like a sore—
> And then run?
> Does it stink like rotten meat:
> Or crust and sugar over—
> Like a syrupy sweet?
> May be it just sags
> Like a heavy load.
> Or does it explode?

is suggestive of the explosive quality of the dreams nurtured by the Younger family—Walter, Mama, Ruth and Beneatha.

The action of the play is set in Chicago's Southside, sometimes between world war II and the present. The play is in three Acts.

The characters are drawn from plain working class. Walter has worked as a chauffeur most of his life, his wife Ruth did domestic work in people's kitchen, so did his mother. Travis, Walter and Ruth's son belongs to the sixth generation of their family in America.

Hansberry's dramas are dominated by women. Motherhood is the centre of appeal, the play is a representation of what it means to love as a mother and to be a black American woman. The three female characters in the play are strongly portrayed, Mama, Mrs Lena Younger, is a woman in her early sixties, full bodied and strong. Being a woman who had adjusted to many things in life and overcome many more, her face is full of strength. Ruth, about thirty, must have been a pretty girl but when the play starts, disappointment has already begun to hang in her face. Beneatha is about twenty, as slim and intense as her brother Walter. She is not as pretty as her sister-in-law, Ruth, but her lean, almost intellectual face has a handsomeness of its own.

The central interest of the play hinges on a cheque which Mama is expecting from her husband's Insurance money. She takes a firm decision, negating her son Walter's dream of setting up a liquor shop.

> Mama: (Quietly) I don't low no yellin' in this house, Walter Lee, and you know it—And there ain't going to be no investing in no liquor stores. I don't aim to have to speak on that again.[1]

Thus explicitly stating who's at the helm of affairs at home.

The play articulates the anxieties and aspirations of three black women, projected by mama (Mrs. Lena Younger), who has lived through difficult times: "In my time we was worried about not being lynched and getting to the north if we could and how to stay alive and still have a pinch of dignity too" (392). She cherishes a dream of owning a house:

> A nice house. Three bedrooms nice big one for you and Ruth [...]. And a little yard with a patch of dirt where I could maybe get to grow me a few flowers [...]. And a nice big basement. (399)

Ruth also shares Mama's dream of owning a nice house.

Beneatha, the youngest of the three is completely disillusioned with the Integrationist principles. She declares:

> I hate assimilationist Negroes [...]. It means someone who is willing to give up his own culture and submerge himself completely in the dominant, and in this case, oppresive culture. (395)

She is infuriated when George Murchison, her boyfriend tells her that "your heritage is nothing but a bunch of raggedly assed spirituals and some grasshuts" (395). She defiantly retorts: "See there [...] you are standing there in your splendid ignorance talking about people who were the first to smelt iron on the face of the earth. The Ashanti were performing surgical operations when the English were still tattooing themselves with blue dragons" (395).

Thus she determinedly demonstrates the supremacy of

the black civilization. She too has a dream, a dream of becoming a doctor:

> I always thought it was one concrete thing in the world that a human being could do. Fix up the sick, you know—and make them whole again. This was truly being God. (415)

Among those troublesome, marginalized issues, is the pregnancy of Ruth. She finds no joy in the prospect of bringing another child into the grim and potentially explosive world, makes plans for an abortion. When Ruth's husband Walter expresses his disbelief about Ruth trying to get rid of the child, Mama knowingly says: "When the world gets ugly enough—a woman will do anything for her family. The part that's already living" (392). However, she does not have an abortion in the end.

The play is powerfully sustained by the suffering, endurance and dreams of these three women. Mama (Mrs Lena Younger), in a bid to retrieve some of the lost happiness of the Younger family goes out and buys a house from her husband's Insurance money. Justifying the need for a house, she tells her son Walter:

> Son—you—you understand what I done, don't you? I—I just seen my family falling apart today [...] just falling to pieces in front of my eyes [...]. We couldn't of gone on like we were today. We were going backwards stead of forwards—talking bout killing babies and wishing each other was dead [...] when it gets like that in life you just got to do something different, push on out and do something bigger. (400)

But when she realizes that she has butchered up her son's dream, she says: "There ain't nothing worth holding on to, money, dreams, nothing else—if it means—if it means its going to destroy my boy" (403). For Ruth the purchase of the house is like a dream come true, she raises both her arms classically and makes an attempt to pacify her husband: "please, honey let me be glad [...] you be glad too [...] oh, Walter, a home [...] a home" (399).

The family witnesses disillusionment of their cherished dreams. Walter's dream of a liquor shop, Beneatha's of becoming a doctor goes to dust when Walter messes up the money by foolishly trusting the unscrupulous Willy with his money.

The euphoria of the new house is also shattered, one week later when the Younger family receives a caller Mr. Karl Linder, a representative of the Clybourne Park Improvement Association, who had come in a bid to buy the house from the family at financial gain to the family, in order to restrain the coloured family from occupying a house in a white community. When Mama wants to know if they were threatened, Beneatha's bitterness spills out: "oh-Mama—They don't do it like that any more, he talked Brotherhood. He said everybody ought to learn how to sit down and hate each other with good Christian fellowship" (409). In the play's conclusion, Walter regains his dignity by informing the white man that the Youngers have changed their minds and will move into their house in the white neighbourhood. In spite of all the reverses of fate, Ruth has tenaciously clung to her dream of moving out and with an urgency and desperation makes a fierce declaration at the end of play:

> I'll strap my baby on back if I have to and scrub all the floors in America and wash all the sheets in America if I have to—but we got to move we got to get out of here (418). "Let's GET THE HELL OUT OF HERE!" (422)

This landmark of black women's drama presents a vision of a theatre and a world informed by what Raymond Williams has called "a new tragic consciousness."[2] This play represents the position of all those who, appalled by the present, are for this reason firmly committed to a different future: to the struggle against suffering learned in suffering: a total exposure which is also a total involvement. To fulfil this vision black women's dramas re-create world's past and present in terms of a redefined notion of heritage and inspire our conviction that things could, indeed, be different.

NOTES

1. Lorraine Hansberry, "A Raisin in the Sun," in R.F. Dietrich, William E. Carpenter and Kevin Kerrane (eds.), *The Art of Modern Drama* (NY: Holt, Rinehart and Winston Inc., 1969) 390. All subsequent references to this work are given parenthetically.
2. Raymond Williams, *Modern Tragedy* (Stanford: Stanford University Press, 1966) 54.

4

POETRY AS A 'THERAPEUTIC PROCESS': SYLVIA PLATH AND KAMALA DAS

NANDINI SAHU

Love, as a theme of poetry has never escaped poets—be it the idyllic love of Shakespearean plays, or the classical platonic love, or even the down-to-earth erotic love. Women play a major role in the game of love. She is more sensitive about love than her counterpart. She forgets her identity, completely merges with her lover. A woman gets the jolt of her life when her tender world of imagination gets shattered being deceived in love. Failure in love as a theme is more powerful in the poetry of confessional poets than its consummation. The whole volumes of the poetry of Kamala Das and Sylvia Plath revolve around this theme, either directly or indirectly. One may take the cases of poets like Sylvia Plath, Anne Sexton, Adrienne Rich, Caroline Kizer, Joy Harjo, Leslie Marmon Silko in America and Kamala Das, Gouri Deshpande, Mamata Kalia, Meena Alexander and many others in India who created a tradition of love poetry as a historical alternative to calm down the utter frustration in their heart and soul. They may differ in their contexts, aesthetics, their poetic output, but the basic poetic stuff of all of them is the perception and experience as women and as poets. For them, poetry is a medium of intimate revelation leading towards personal salvation, redemption. It is a therapeutic process, a way of coming to terms with the exceptional female energy that lies in their inner self.

Kamala Das gives a new dimension to love poetry by revealing her kinship with an interior Indian tradition which has its roots in Indian epics. Apart from this, her Nayar background provides a suitable plot to her to modify her

Indianised tone into multiple facets of poetry. Kamala Das's love poetry can be divided into two phases—the first phase deals with her obsessive concern with the physical and the metaphysical while the second phase drifts her towards the ideal and the platonic love. P. Mallikarjuna Rao views:

> Kamala Das's love poems stand apart as they fruitfully combine the indigenous traditions such as 'Abhisarika' and 'Sahaja' and the confessional tradition which is western. Her love poetry is a fine blending of two different literary traditions.

Kamala Das's shocking confessions about her numerous love episodes have startled the readers and the critics as well. It is more shocking because it comes from an Indian woman. Das started seeking love and sexual experience when she was an adolescent. She records her yearnings in her autobiography *My Story* thus:

> I was looking for an ideal lover. I was looking for the one who went to Mathura and forgot to return to his Radha. Perhaps I was seeking the cruelty that lies in the depths of a man's heart. Otherwise why did I not get my peace in the arms of my husband?

Das's search for love in more than one person leads her to more complexities. Her advantage of being a modern poet is that she can discuss 'love' and 'sex' without any inhibitions. She is able to present her raw, naked themes without clothing them with symbols, imagery or metaphors. She talks with utmost candour in "The Freaks":

> [...] our minds
> Are willed to race towards love;
> But they only wander, tripping
> Idly over puddles of
> Desire [...] Can't this man with
> Nimble finger tips unleash
> Nothing more alive than the
> Skin's lazy hungers? Who can
> Help us who have lived so long
> And have failed in love? [...].
> I am a freak. It's only

To save my face, I flaunt, at
Times a grand, flamboyant lust. ("The Freaks")

Her urge for love becomes intense which can be traced in her poetic growth. Many persons entered her life as lovers, freedom was her "dancing shoe," and she does not make efforts to hide it:

Love became a swivel-door,
When one went out, another came in
Then I lost count, for always in my arms
Was a substitute for a substitute. ("Substitute")

Being deceived by her husband and all her lovers Das writes:

Oh yes, getting
A man to love is easy, but living
Without him afterwards may have to be
Faced. ("The Looking Glass")

Her experiments with love take many turns and in the course gives birth to more frustrations and more poetry. She wanted a love of her ideas and became a prisoner in that gladly:

As the convict studies
His prison's geography
I study the trappings
Of your body, dear love,
For I must someday find
An escape from its snare. ("The Prisoner")

Das was sick of the love, which is just skin deep. With her strong aversion to lust, she questions:

[…] What is
The use, what is the bloody use?
That was the only kind of love
This hacking at each other's parts
Like convicts hacking, breaking clods
At noon [...]. ("Convicts")

Her ideal love,—which she sought in her grandmother's love, her parental love and also the soft lesbian love which she had experienced at 'school—is quite contradictory to the love she writes about in "The Old Playhouse." She had to suffer incessantly in gratifying the male sexuality:

You called me wife
I was taught to break saccharine into your tea and
To offer at the right moment the vitamins. Cowering
Beneath your monstrous ego I ate the magic loaf and
Became a dwarf. ("The Old Playhouse")

In nourishing the male with vitamins, the female personae succumbs into a weakling, offers him sexual gratification when desired. The trapping of the swallow suggests that marriage is a kind of social entrapment.

Das mythologizes her search for true love and identifies herself with Radha or Mira Bai who relinquished the marital ties in search of Lord Krishna, the true and eternal lover:

Vrindavan lives on in every women's minds,
and the flute, luring her
From home and her husband
Who later asks her of the long scratch on the brown
Aureola of her breast, and she slyly replies,
hiding flushed cheeks
It was so dark outside, I tripped and fell over
the brambles in the wood. ("Radha Krishna")

Anyway, in her love for Krishna the element of 'bhakti' is missing, and her yearning for Krishna is purely human. She lives in two worlds at a time, the actual world where love is usually associated with lust and the legendary world which is a spiritual world, where a union with God is desired. This is illustrated by the poem "Radha" where she somewhat sentimentally depicts the ecstasy that Radha experiences in Krishna's arms:

Everything in me
is melting, even hardness at core
O Krishna, I am melting, melting
Nothing remains but
You [...]

But Radha does not break her marital ties as she considers the body insignificant. The poem "Maggots" embodies Radha's experience with her husband, which is analogous with Das's married life, indifferent, cold:

At sunset, on the river bank, Krishna
Loved her for the last time and left [...]
That night in her husband's arms Radha felt
So dead that he asked, what is wrong
Do you mind my kisses, love? And she said,
No, not at all, but thought, what is
It to the corpse if the maggots nip? ("Maggots")

Krishna plays a therapeutic role in the poet's life, in the love of whom she gets relief from the pangs of male chauvinism.

Kamala Das, like Sylvia Plath, had an encounter with death, but luckily she was saved from its fierce grip. Her quest for love continues to be the theme of her poetry which projects her as an optimist. Her bold expressions of frenzied love got her both appreciations and criticism. She never admits to be a nymphomaniac and denies that her poems are pornographic in tone. Regarding her extreme sentimentalism, E.V. Ramakrishnan says, "Compared to the poems of Anne Sexton, Sylvia Plath and Theodore Roethke, the poems of Kamala Das lack in the unifying stream that has to run through the various shifting moods. Her poems are wanting in a patient writing and delivering of thoughts in a spontaneous rhythm. At the level of ideas her poems are extremely compressed dynamic wholes on the verge of bursting."

Sylvia Plath, too, has handled the theme of love in a brilliant way. The self-pity in Das's poems is completely absent in Plath's poetry and she has very few poems on the theme of love as compared to Das. Plath was born and brought up in an intellectual atmosphere. She was a very talented teenager with all 'A' grades behind her. She would not be at ease with her own age group who went out on dates and discussed them with excitement. The emotional void created by her father's untimely death and mother's involvement in her own career made the poet an introvert. For a few years, her intellectual achievements and the scholarships she won were mistaken for a substitute to love. But soon she got a need in her life to assert herself as a full-blooded woman. As a teenager in the College she adored a few boys but it was only infatuation. In her confessional novel *Bell Jar* she records her experiences with Buddy Williard as mere infatuation.

In their introduction to "Psyche: The Feminine Poetic Consciousness" (1973) Barbara Segnitz and Carol Rainey view that love and a conflict between passivity and rebellion against the male-dominated society is the major preoccupation of the women poets. Sylvia Plath is concerned with failures in love, "the unbearability of being a woman, and a search for love that is secure, mature, perfect. Plath's poems are basically concerned with human identity, but she effectively uses the rhetorical modes in order to focus pertinent questions relating to a woman's identity in a male-dominated world. Plath has perfected a way of treating the most intimate experience without ever being sentimental or showing any trace of pathos. In her poems one can assume the voice of the new liberated women even if she prefers speaking on behalf of everybody but herself. Her frank admissions and bold treatment of private life prove her to be the best confessional poet. In her poems she uses a series of shifting moods and voices within voices. She lays bare her failures, ignorance, hesitations, shame and feelings of guilt in the poems who project her personality. The poets who are mostly called confessional poets are Theodore Roethke, Anne Sexton, John Berryman, Plath, Allen Ginsberg and Snodgrass. All these poets have in common a capacity for ruthless self-analysis and a tone of utter sincerity.

Following her suicide in 1963 and the posthumous publication of her work a great deal of critical attention has been focused on the art of Sylvia Plath. Her 696 letters, which are genuinely fruitful, spontaneous and straight-forward, edited with loving care by her mother, reveal her complex character with a pathetic bewilderment. Plath's psychological difficulties flowed from a pronounced Electra complex of which she confesses in one of her uncollected poems:

> Oh pardon the one who knocks for pardon at
> Your gate, father—Your bound-bitch, daughter, friend
> It was my love that died us both to death.
>
> ("Electra on the Azelea Path")

The twin themes of love and death are interwoven in her works as two recurring motifs. Plath's first encounter with death came at the age of eight with her father's death when she said, "I'll never speak to God again." And a pathological fascination with death appears in her novel and her poems later on. For Plath, love is a sense of well-being, not a romantic passion. Plath always associates death with love:

> Dying
> is an art, like everything else
> I do it exceptionally well. ("Lady Lazarus." *Ariel*)

There is a notion in her poetry that the poet seeks death because she loves life; for her suicide was her "last act of love" ("Letters Home"). All the poems written by Plath including her posthumous collection *Ariel* can be grouped under love poems. She is in love with Nature, sea, her father, lover, and with death itself. Plath was utterly disillusioned with the concept of love, as a result love in the normal sense of the term is conspicuously absent in her poetry. In "Courtier" she says about love:

> Don't accept it. It is not genuine
> A ring of gold with the sun in it
> Lies, lies, and a grief. ("Courtier")

She had a strong resentment towards marriage. The poem "The Applicant" ridicules male ego who treat woman as "it":

> Here is a hand
> To fill it and willing
> To bring teacups and roll away headache
> And do whatever you tell it,
> Will you marry it?

The reduction of the female personality is brought out by the repetition of "it":

> Will you marry it?
> It is waterproof, shatterproof, proof
> Against fire and bombs through the roof.
> [...] Will you marry it, marry it, marry it?

The proof against water, fire, shatter shows the applicant's desire in marrying a better woman than a fragile one who would show up better in growing years unlike a real woman. Ironic refrain comes out with a seemingly convincing logic and persuasive logic:

> In twenty-five years she'll be silver
> In fifty, gold.

A living doll, everywhere you look.
It can talk, talk, talk.
It works, there's nothing wrong with it.

The female personae is no more than a rubber doll, a sex-object. In the poem Plath speaks violently in terms of love offered by a male:

The strong man's technique is
Always the same, he serves his love in lethal doses,
For, love is Narcissus at the water's edge, haunted
By its own lonely face, and yet it must seek at last
An end, a pure total freedom, it must will the mirrors
To shatter and the kind night to erase the water.

The metaphor Narcissus speaks of man's self-love. Plath's search for the right man to share her love and life comes to an end when she meets Ted Hughes and gets married to him in 1956. Both being creative writers with similar tastes in life and literature, allows one to predict a happy married life, which comes round on quite a contradictory way. Plath's world enlarges when she becomes a mother and successfully pursues her home and career. She says:

One cry, and I stumble from bed,
cow-heavy and floral
In my Victorian night gown.

She confesses of her broken marriage to her son. After Plath's motherhood, Hughes's initial fascination started getting worn off and he developed affairs with other women which broke her heart and she got separated from him. That was the end of her love life. Ted Hughes takes her for granted and claims that as an intellectual he is sure to have such affairs which she must bear. Plath writes:

I am not a mystical: it isn't
As if I thought it had a spirit,
It is simply in its elements. ("Pleasant")

Now she madly loves her children, takes rescue in their love:

Love, love
I have hung our cave with roses,
With soft rugs—
The last of Victoriana. ("You are the baby in the barn.")

Her only alternative was to fall in love with Death which seemed to have attracted her since long, and which is manifested in the regular suicidal attempts of the personae in the *Bell Jar*. She gets cynical about love and writes:

> Love, the World
> Suddenly turns, turns colour. ("Letter in November")

And again,

> The heart shuts
> The sea slides back
> The mirror is sheeted.

To these poets, writing poems on love and frustration is just an alternative to attaining true love in real life. In this context one may quote Devendra Kohli who writes, "To a great extent confessional poetry comes to mean [...] love poetry which is revelatory of intimate details and complex emotions [...]. It is through love poetry that the implicit (and at times the explicit) commentary on male indifference, callousness, insensitivity, exploitation of the female come through."

One might link Kamala Das not only with Plath but with Anne Sexton who is the best example of confessional love poetry. Anne Sexton's volume of poems *Love Poems* and in particular her poems such as "Little Girl, My String Bean, My Lovely Woman," "In Celebration of My Uterus," "For My Lover, Returning to His Wife" celebrate love in its psychological basis. Most women poets have battled against mental breakdowns and suicidal tendencies. Anne Sexton took to writing poetry because it was a course of action prescribed by her psychiatrist. She had been admitted to a mental hospital for the second time in 1956, attempted suicide on November and December she started writing poetry, encouraged by her psychiatrist, Dr. Martin. But this therapeutic element is missing to some extent in the confessional love poetry written in India as sometimes the Indian women poets are biased by excess of emotions.

Both Sylvia Plath and Kamala Das are painfully aware of male hypocrisy and female subjugation. Plath's "Blackberrying," "Strumpet Song," "Fever 103" and Das's "The Freaks," "Composition," "The Old Playhouse" etc. are some of the poems where one can guess how sex repels both of them. Plath says about men, "They are-jealous gods/ That would have the whole World flat because they are;" and Das says, "Falling in love is a dangerous thing. / It is like tying oneself with a rope" ("A Doll for the Child Prostitute"). Both relish a nostalgic fervour which is best expressed in Das's "A Hot Noon in Malabar" and Plath's "All the Dead Dears." Plath's *Bell Jar* may be compared with Das's *Alphabet of Lust* and Das's *My Story* with Plath's "*Letters Home.*" Plath's "October Poems" also known as "Dawn Poems" or a "Fall Poems" written during the Fall of 1962 include deeply moving poems like "Daddy," "Lady Lazarus," "Purdah," "Fever 103," "The Applicant" offer close comparison with Das's powerful poems like "The Freaks," "Gino," "In Love," "The Stone Age," "The Old Playhouse" and several others. In these poems both of them reveal their emotional suffering with remarkable efflorescent in art. The essential difference between the two poets lies in the fact that Das sounds too subjective in her poems while Plath succeeds in achieving complete objectivity, impersonality. Anisur Rahman views, "While in Das's poems the popular distinction between the man who suffers and the artist who creates is seemingly obliterated, in Plath's poems it takes much deeper roots. In Das's poem, progression takes place in terms of 'you' and 'I' whereas in Plath there is an atmosphere of sale and purchase and the poet's persona is nowhere in the foreground."

Both Das and Plath's voice and nature of experience, their spontaneity and expressions on a woman's experience focus on the fact that there has been a heightening of interest in the work of woman poets/writers. More anthologies of woman poets have been brought out recently in U.S.A. and India. The important themes are how a woman writer can redefine herself and the world around her by breaking completely and violently from the traditional roles to be played by women.

Kamala Das, Sylvia Plath, Anne Sexton, Adrinne Rich, Caroline Kizer and most other feminist poets project themes of love and frustration in their poetry. For them love is not a means to an end. Rather love poetry provides them a medium, a historical alternative to challenge a society characterized by dominant, aggressive men and passive, victimized, acquiescent women. Through their love poems they express a distinctively assertive feminine sensibility even if they do not assume any feminine stance, ideology or feminist politics.

NOTES AND REFERENCES

Das, Kamala. *My Story*. New Delhi: Sterling Publication, 1973.

——. *The Old Playhouse and other Poems*. New Delhi: Orient Longman, 1973.

Kohli, Devendra. "Confessional Poetry as Social Commentary: View of Indian Poetry in English by Indian Women Poets. *Contemporary Indian English Poetry*. Ed. Atma Ram. Calcutta: A Writers Workshop Publication, 1989, 55.

"Love is a Shadow" *Indian Journal of American Studies*. Vol. 22, No. 2, Summer 1992, 77.

Plath, Sylvia. *Letters Home*. Ed. Aurelia Schober Plath. London: Faber and Faber, 1975.

——. *Ariel*. London: Faber and Faber, 1965.

"Poetry of Kamala Das," *Triveni*, Vol. 58, No. 2, April-June, 1989, 5.

Ramakrishnan, E.V. "Kamala Das as a Confessional Poet," *The Journal of Indian Writing in English*, Vol. 5, No. l, Jan. 1977, 34.

5

ATWOOD'S 'MUSE': IN THE '[GRAND]MOTHER'S MIRROR'

RAMA KUNDU

I am the old woman
sitting across from you on the bus,
her shoulders drawn up like a shawl;
out of her eyes come secret
hatpins, destroying
the walls, the ceiling

Turn, look down:
There is no city;
this is the centre of a forest...

("A Bus along St Clair: December,"
The Journals of Susanna Moodie)

Here Margaret Atwood envisions in the figure of "the old woman" a visionary/muse who can transport one's mind from the cramping material immediacy to an exciting release into mystery, signified by the wild forest. This is a poem from the section called "Journal III," and the author tells us, "Most of Journal III was written after I had come across a little-known photograph of Susanna Moodie as a mad-looking and very elderly lady" (*JSM* 63). In another poem of the same section the same "very elderly lady" gives voice to her mysterious vision of an oncoming metamorphosis. Her grandchildren can little guess how under the façade of "deafness," "cameo brooch," "puckered mind/ scurrying in its old burrows" she carries the potential for a mystic transmigration right into the springs of life and energy, when she:

> [...] will prowl and slink
> in crystal darkness
> among the stalactite roots, with new
> formed plumage
>   uncorroded
>   gold and
> Fiery green, my fingers
> curving and scaled, my
> opal
>   no
> eyes glowing. ("Wish: Metamorphosis [...]")

For centuries, and millenniums, we have spoken of 'ancestors,' but not of 'ancestresses.' It is this foremother or ancestress, in place of 'forefather' or 'ancestor,' who has been emerging as a new icon in *ecriture feminine* across the globe today. Canada and India being no exception. Helene Cixous would say: "a woman is never far from 'mother' [...] there is always within her at least a little of that good mother's milk. She writes in white ink" (Cixous). Indeed, this reminds us of what Virginia Woolf had said nearly half a century ago, in *A Room of One's Own:* "We think back through our mothers if we are women" (83). Margaret Atwood's concept of "muse" can be understood in this light. As the poet explains in an interview:

> I myself always thought the muse was female [...]. If the muse is a woman for the woman poet, unless the poet is a lesbian, the sexual connection gets removed, and it's more like a second self, a twin, a mother, a wise old woman [...]. That's how we learn to speak, usually from our mothers. (Sullivan 108)

Apparently Atwood does not seem to be very definite about this 'second self.' She can be a sister ("Twin"), mother, or some "old" -er and "wiser" woman, that is, one who has suffered more and experienced more. But in whatever image she may surface times and again, it is basically the idea of an 'other' woman within the writer who seems to motivate, inspire, and mould her writing. As one goes through Atwood's poems one feels how this 'other' within the self becomes increasingly a conglomerate image which becomes a contraction and coinciding point of generations of women. One may cite the following lines from "Five Poems for Grandmothers":

> Sons branch out, but
> one woman leads to another.
> Finally I know you
> through your daughters,
> my mother, her sisters,
> and through myself. (*Selected Poems II* 14)

This assertion—or better to say, wishful thinking—of a common heritage,—of a matrilineal line of ancestry[1] and belonging may have been prompted by the author's perception of the woman's alienation, even as a writer. While the male poets in their common journey enjoy a degree of sharing, the women remain isolated; this is how Atwood perceives the "pilgrimage" in her poem "The Words Continue their Journey."

> I see us, travelling together,
> the women veiled and singly, with that inturned
> sight and the eyes averted,
> the men in groups, with their moustaches
> and passwords and bravado. (*Selected Poems II* 116)

It is the urgency of overcoming this alienation that governs the poet's search for her own myth, which should recognise and acknowledge and project "the long thread" connecting mothers who had been daughters, to their dead mothers, and their growing daughters, who in their turn will be mothers to their daughters. As she writes in "A Red Shirt":

> This is the procession
> of old leathery mothers, [...]
> passing the work from hand to hand,
> mother to daughter,
> a long thread of red blood, not yet broken.
> (*Selected Poems II* 48)

The image of "leather" in Atwood is associated with compulsive/ enforced silence,—that of the woman burnt alive on the charge of witchery, "her mouth covered by leather/ to strangle words" ("Spelling" *True Stories* 64). The mother in this poem envisions her daughter playing with plastic letters, "learning how to spell,/ spelling,/ how to make spells." She feels that the conventional education of grammar and spelling will be an incomplete lesson for her daughter; it would not help her tear the leather from the mouth. Instead, she must pass on to her another language of instinctive wisdom:

> At the point where language falls away
> from the hot bones, at the point
> where the rock breaks open and darkness
> flows out of it like blood.

The poem concludes with an exhortation to the small daughter for asserting her identity:

> How do you learn to spell?
> Blood, sky & the sun,
> your own name first,
> your first naming, your first name,
> your first word.

This is the wisdom,—the painful message to assert herself—that the mother can impart to her daughter, so that she can give her own fight when the time comes:

> I would like to say, Dance
> and be happy. Instead I will say
> in my *crone's* voice, Be [emphasis added]
> ruthless when you have to, tell
> the truth when you can,
> when you can see it. ("Solstice Poem," *Selected Poems II)*

The meaning of the figure of the "witch" or "crone" in Atwood's poems thus gets defamiliarised, and wrenched from their traditional/conventional contexts. Mary Webster in "Half-Hanged Mary" speaks in the voice of a woman who has marginally averted death by hanging on charge of using witchcraft:

> Before, I was not a witch.
> But now I am one. [...]
> I speak in tongues, [...]
> The words boil out of me,
> Coil after coil of sinuous possibility.
> The cosmos unravels from my mouth.
> All fullness, all vacancy. (*Morning*)

Classical myths prove inadequate to meet the need of the situation. Atwood's Euridyce is the unrecognized alien, reduced to an "echo" by her lover; she accuses Orpheus: "You could not believe I was more than your echo" ("Orpheus" *Selected Poems II*). Helen is the fantasized and slandered whore, for whom the choice finally comes down to selling lures only:

> Like preachers, I sell vision,
> like perfume ads, desire
> or its facsimile. [...]
> I sell men back their worst suspicions:
> That everything's for sale,
> And piecemeal.
>
> ("Helen of Troy does Counter Dancing," *Morning*)

Instead she finds in the traditionally despised, because feared, figures—the crone, the so-called witch, the old hag—the outspoken outcast, an appropriate icon of female wisdom. It is to this icon that she turns in her search for the matrilineal heritage, "the thread of blood" running down the endless line of mothers-daughters-mothers. The poetic muse thus becomes manifest to her in "the crone's voice," in the 'witch's' "tongues," in the wizened utterance of the old matriarch.

At this point one must take note of the fact that Atwood does not sentimentalise the much-lauded maternal instinct which is also a patriarchal construct, imposed in terms of "should[s]" and "should not[s]" to subjugate women, and to instill bad faith in them to embrace, without question, the role of the sacrificial heifer:

> women should not contemplate war, [...]
> Women should march for peace,
> or hand out white feathers to arouse bravery,
> spit themselves on bayonets
> to protect their babies [...]
> or, having been raped repeatedly,
> hang themselves with their own hair.
>
> ("The Loneliness of the Military Historian," *Morning*)

The poet draws out the subversive element in the folkloric myths which undermine the valorised myth of the self-effacing, self-sacrificing mother, in a poem which itself reads like an argument:

> Of course there are mothers
> squeezing their breasts

dry, pawning their bodies,
shedding teeth for their children,
or that's our fond belief.
But remember—Hansel
And Gretel were dumped in the forest
because their parents were starving.
("Red Fox," *Morning*)

The poet thus questions the 'institution' of motherhood along with its enforced roles on women.

Atwood's imagination is stirred by the figure of Susanna Moodie[2] because the woman, an "ancestress" to the Canadian woman writer, seems to represent the earthy female wisdom of the "crone" or the "witch" [in the Atwood sense] who has attained a mysterious communion with Nature and Life and Death. The "witch" or "crone" or "old Hag" becomes merged into the silent "unknown twin," who waits inside her brain, and gives solidity to her utterances. She is "The Signer":

In an area of darkness behind my head
stands a woman dressed in black,
[...] my unknown twin. [...]
In her hands, deft as a knitter's
but quicker, my words turn solid,
become a gesture, a skein,
a semaphore of the body. (*Morning*)

The shadow in the mirror is of the "unknown," yet instinctively known, being a "twin"; it is mysterious, yet part of the other twin's own self. Luce Irigaray proposes a feminist narcissism in order to subvert the power of patriarchy to hold the gaze in which woman is seen only as man would see her, in his image, or as a mirror reflection of his gaze. In the title section of her book *Speculum of the Other Woman* (trans. 1985) Irigaray describes the central problematic of woman's attempt to resolve in harmony her female interconnections, and in this connection questions the validity of the antifeminist narcissism assumed by the Lacanian mirror:

> Are we to assume that a mirror has always already been inserted, and speculates every perception and conception of the world, with the exception of itself, whose reflection would only be a factor of time? Thus

> extension would always already be re-staged and re-projected by the subject who, alone, would not be situated there. Does the subject derive his power from the appropriation of this non-place of the mirror? And from speculation? And as speculation constitutes itself as such in this way, it cannot be analyzed. (Irigaray: 1985, 205)

Atwood refuses to allow this non-space in her 'mirror' to be appropriated; rather she would restore it to her 'unknown twin' who merges into the 'mother' who again merges into the 'grandmother,' the 'crone,' the 'witch.' Thus she takes up the "new challenge" which Irigaray tried to formulate in her thoughts on "Women's Exile" (1977):

> The fact remains: the relationship of women to their mothers and to other women—thus towards themselves—are subject to total narcissistic "black out"; these relationships are completely devalued. Indeed, I have never come across a woman who does not suffer from the problem of not being able to resolve in harmony, in the present system, her relationship with her mother and with other women. Psychoanalysis has totally mythologised and "censored" the positive value of these relationships. (Irigaray: 1977, 75)

Atwood's poems show an attempt at demythologising these relationships and restoring them to their positive value by means of invoking the female 'muse' as the mother, grandmother, ancestress, witch, crone, old hag, and one's 'unknown twin' sister in the 'mirror' of self-discovery, even if the progress towards the mirror,[3] getting an access to it, involves a tenuous and painful process. The first poem in the journals of Atwood's Susanna Moodie, "Disembarking at Quebec," shows the ancestress arriving at the perception of the inadequacy of a conventional mirror: "The moving water will not show me/ my reflection." The necessary dislocation in the life of an immigrant woman enables her to re-examine the validity of the inherited mirror, and leads subsequently to her rejection of "a mirror," and opting for the "wolf's eyes" instead ("Further Arrivals"). Eventually, after years of "roughing it up" in the lonely "wilderness," she stumbles upon her own mirror, and boldly grasps it, however unflattering it may be. The discussion may be concluded by citing the exclamation of the thrashed, stiffened, hardened figure of the foremother,—Susanna Moodie,—as she looks into her own mirror;[4] seven years in the prairie have led to crushed face, stained skin, stiff limbs, brittle fingers, cracked mouth; still it is important to look into the mirror:

> you find (in the mirror) only
> the shape you already are
> but what
> if you have forgotten that
> or discover you
> have never known. ("Looking in a Mirror," *Journal*)

Postscript: Atwood's 1976 novel *Lady Oracle,* a work acutely conscious as it is of its own status within the problematic category of 'women's writing,' makes an elaborate use of the 'mirror.' The novel opens with Joan narrating in the past tense the events leading up to her own death:

> I planned my death carefully; unlike my life, which meandered along from one thing to another, despite my feeble efforts to control it. My life had a tendency to spread, to get flabby, to scroll and festoon like the frame of a baroque *mirror,* which came from following the line of least resistance. I wanted my death, by contrast, to be neat and simple. (3; emphasis added)

The fantasy figure of 'Lady Oracle,'—who is also the Joan's third "self," the other two being her self-chosen shapes of the slim attractive female, and the dull cook-cum-nurse—came into being as Joan pieced together words she had written during passages of self-hypnosis. Significantly, it is a mirror through which Joan enters the subterranean region of the 'lady oracle'; the mirror is, again, a replication of the three-sided mirror of her childhood, in which she had seen her mother as a hydra-headed "monster" (70). As Molly Hite rightly perceives, "The device of the mirror as entry suggests that the powerful, unhappy, somehow maternal persona of the poem is the reverse or repressed side of the 'happy and inept' persona (248) that Joan allows herself and is allowed by the society" (147). Joan remembers:

> [...] my mother always had a triple mirror, so she could see both sides as well as the front of her head. In the dream, as I watched, I suddenly realized that instead of three reflections she had three actual heads, which rose from her toweled shoulders on three separate necks. This did not frighten me, as it seemed merely a confirmation of something I had always known; [...] her secret, the secret I alone knew: my mother was a monster. (70)

Molly Hite comments:

> [...] the mirrors that allow her mother to make herself into the requisite object of masculine desire, and thus to make herself into an exemplary mirror that will reflect back exactly what the phallocentric culture wishes to see, are transformed by the dream into portals leading to the revelation of feminine monstrosity, of woman as irreducibly multiple. In Joan's experiments with automatic writing, the triple mirrors lead into a labyrinth identified both with the unconscious and with the maternal. (161)

In the nightmarish dystopian world of Atwood's 1985 novel, *The Handmaid's Tale,* where the women are reduced at gunpoint to the status of mere breeding machine, mirrors have become scarce. The narrator finds one remaining mirror on the hall wall of the Commander's house, where she is being used as a 'womb'; she finds only a grotesque distortion there which but mocks herself:

> There remains a mirror, on the hall wall. [...] I can see it as I go down the stairs, round, convex, a pier-glass, like the eye of a fish, and myself in it like a distorted shadow, a parody of something [...]. (19)

The mirrors here, can show, in addition to the distorted self-image, sinister intrusions of oppressive outsiders into one's privacy. Even when 'Offred' rides up in the elevator towards the doctor's chamber, she is 'escorted' by the police spy. "In the black mirror wall of the elevator I can see the back of his head" (69). Or when the 'Commander's wife, desperate for a baby, forces 'Offred' to seek surreptitious copulation with a younger man, she sees "the two of us, a blue shape, a red shape, in the brief glass eye of the mirror as we descend. Myself, my obverse" (271). Only once she gets the chance of looking in an "ample mirror under the white light" in the exclusive brothel to which she is taken by the 'Commander,' and in the "good look, slow and level" in the toilette mirror she learns, "I'm a wreck" (265).

NOTES

1. Way back in 1932 Dorothy Livesay (b. 1909) makes a loving, nostalgic invocation to the 'grandmother' in her poem "Green Rain." As memory surges back, the image of the grandmother becomes the overwhelming sign of all that had been dear and treasured:

   I remember long veils of green rain
   Feathered like the shawl of my grandmother [...]
   I remember the road [...]
   [...] which leads to my grandmother's house,
   A warm house [...]
   And the silence, full of the rain's falling
   Was like my grandmother's parlour
   Alive with herself and her voice, rising and falling—
   Rain and wind intermingled. [...]
   Now I remember the day
   As I remember my grandmother.
   I remember the rain as the leathery fringe of her shawl.

   [*The New Oxford Book of Canadian Verse* 134]

It may also be interesting to recall in this context the following lines from Sylvia Plath's "All the Dead Dears" (*The Colossus*):

   From the mercury backed glass
   Mother, grandmother, great grandmother
   Reach me, hug hands to have me in.

2. Elizabeth Brewster's (b. 1922) poem "Great-Aunt Rebecca" (1969) re-creates through "remembering" another Susanna Moodie figure, and evokes a grandmother figure of the pioneering generation who becomes the personal idol for her modern granddaughter:

   [...] I too
   Wished to be a pioneer,
   To walk on snowshoes through remote pastures
   [...]; to be like Aunt Rebecca,
   Soft as silk and tough as that thin wire
   They use for snaring rabbits. [*The NOBCV* 224]

3. Atwood's 'mirror' is distinct from the conventional psychiatrist's mirror [*a la* Lacan] or the

   aesthetic 'mirror game' of Durrell—his use of multiple mirrors towards achieving "prism-sightedness" by means of a continuous fracturing of perspectives.

One may also cite Sylvia Plath's poem "Mirror" (*Crossing the Water*):

> Now I am a lake. A woman bends over me,
> Searching my reaches for what she really is.

4. This can be compared and contrasted to the desperate groping of the hangman's bride in Atwood's poem "Marrying the Hangman" (1978) for any mirror which ultimately lands her up in a male mirror, and consequently, from one locked room to another:

> To live in prison is to live without mirrors. To live without mirrors is to live without the self. She is living selflessly, she finds a hole in the stone wall and on the other side of the wall a voice. The voice comes through darkness and has no voice. This voice becomes her mirror [...]
>
> What did she say when she discovered that she had left one locked room for another? [*The NOBCV* 352-54]

Mention may also be made to Jean Rhys's elaborate use of the 'mirror' as a trope in *Wide Sargasso Sea* (1966); Antoinette, living in her attic prison in Rochester's manor house is denied a mirror, and finds no answer to her obsessive puzzle: "Who am I?" Finally she gets the answer when in the mirror of the dream pool she recognises Tia, the black girlfriend of her childhood in the islands, "as if, I saw myself. Like in a looking glass" (38).

REFERENCES

Atwood, M. *The Journals of Susanna Moodie.* Toronto: OUP, 1970.

——. *Lady Oracle.* New York: Avon, 1976.

——. *True Stories.* Toronto: OUP, 1981.

——. *The Handmaid's Tale.* Vintage, 1985.

——. *Selected Poems II: Poems Selected and New 1976-1986.* Boston: Houghton Miffin, 1987.

——. *Morning in the Burned House.* Toronto: McClelland & Stewart, 1995.

——, ed. *The New Oxford Book of Canadian Verse in English.* Toronto; London; N.Y.: OUP, 1982.

Cixous, Helene. "The Laugh of the Medusa." 1976.

Hite, Molly. *The Other Side of the Story.* Ithaca and London: Cornell Univ. Press, 1989.

Irigaray, L. "Women's Exile." Trans. Couze Venn, *Ideology and Consciousness,* I (1977) 75.

——. *Speculum of the Other Woman.* Trans. Gilliam C. Gill. N.Y.: Cornell Univ. Press, 1985.

Rhys, Jean. *Wide Sargasso Sea.* (1966) New York: Penguin Books, 1977.

Sullivan, R. *The Red Shoes: Margaret Atwood Starting Out.* Toronto: Harper Collins, 1998.

Woolf, V. *A Room of One's Own.* (1929) Flamingo: Harper Collins Publishers, 1994.

6

KAMALA MARKANDAYA'S *NECTAR IN A SIEVE*: A REAPPRAISAL

SANTWANA HALDAR

A serious charge brought against Indian writing in English is that the Indian writers in English being urban or suburban, the inclusion of the agrarian, who still form 70 per cent of the total Indian population, is a rare occurrence, and those rare cases, too, are often an outsider's viewpoint. Ironically, then, the so-called subaltern studies which have recently become a craze, are rendered meaningless, as the real subaltern or the marginalised are yet to speak.[1] Kamala Markandaya's *Nectar in a Sieve* (1954) was, however, an exception, and since its publication it has been applauded in home and abroad as a faithful portrait of rural India.[2]

The novel offers not only a vivid description of the hopes and disappointments of an agrarian couple in colonial India, but also a woman protagonist, wife of a tenant farmer. The protagonist Rukmani is doubly marginalized. In feminist discourse, woman is marginalized and man is the centre, irrespective of the economic status of the family. From the Marxist point of view, the proletariat are the peripheral who seek to subvert the bourgeois who are the 'centre.' Rukmani being a woman as well as a proletariat, may be called doubly marginalized. But Kamala Markandaya is least affected either by the feminist or by the Marxist discourse. Rather she produced a saga of a tenant farmer's family through the version of the farmer's wife who was taught how to read and write by her father, a village headman. The plight of the tenant farmers in British India, a total lack of modern infrastructure in the agriculture sector, the farmer's abject poverty, humiliation and a constant fear of being uprooted, the torture inflicted by the local landlord and their agents on the tenant farmers,— all these are vividly portrayed in the novel, and the author is regarded as "one of the major novelists of the commonwealth scene."[3] The novel, yet, raises some serious questions. Is it possible for the protagonist to express herself and her surrounding properly in English? Can a village woman like Rukmani analyse her emotion and maintain a detached attitude to the events of life? Is not the sense of wonder as revealed in Rukmani's joy of producing vegetables, a romanticised version? Rukmani also contradicts herself on some occasions. Lastly, the writer does not make any analysis of the colonial presence in the novel. Dr. Kenny's role as a benefactor is suggestive of while hegemony. The present article intends to raise some of such issues while offering a brief critical analysis of the text.

Broadly speaking, *Nectar in a Sieve* centres on hunger. As a harrowing tale of agrarian bankruptcy it captures the reader's mind and keeps up the suspense till the end. The socio-economic factors in the life of the peasants in colonial India are revealed as tragic forces in the life of Rukmani who takes up all her misfortunes as challenges and faces them in a calm and quiet way, without any protest against the landlord and the almighty. It is the emphasis on fate in the Hindu culture that keeps marginalised groups such as women and the lower classes in India from challenging their subordinate position in the society. Markandaya has also taken up themes like child marriage and barrenness which are closely linked to the initial themes of poverty in the agrarian life. The society to which Rukmani belongs—a village in South India— is free from 'Purdah.' In the novel her life of struggle has been compared to the life of some Muslim women who were financially well off, but had to be cloistered behind the purdah.

The title 'Nectar in a Sieve' suggests the fleeting moments of bliss in Rukmani's life. The youngest daughter of a village headman, Rukmani dreamt of a grand wedding until she learnt that the headman was no longer of consequence:

> There is the collector, who comes to these villages once a year, and to him is the power, and to these he appoints; not to the headman. (2)

The replacement of the traditional village headman by the agents of the colonial power is hinted at. For Rukmani, it was as if the prop on which she had leaned, was roughly kicked away. She was crestfallen when she was given in marriage to Nathan, a tenant farmer. Her knees gave in as she entered her husband's home, "a mud hut, thatched, small, set near a paddy field." But her initial shock being over, she got herself adjusted to her new life. Nathan's words of encouragement, tenderness and love for Rukmani, opened up a new vista for her. She learnt that a farmer's happiness cannot be equated to material prosperity. It is the peace of mind that goes unmatched when one's hands are full of grains and the field one has cultivated, is green. This 'peace' is the nectar that Rukmani was eager to possess, and ironically, these moments of peace flickered, as if the nectar was put on a sieve. And yet, Rukmani is endowed with the capacity to go along the rugged path of life with those moments of peace in her memory:

> While the sun shines on you and the fields are green and beautiful to the eye, and your husband sees beauty in you which no one has seen before, and you have a good store of grain laid away for hard times, a roof over you and a sweet stirring in your body, what more can a woman ask for? My heart sang and my feet were light as I went about my work, getting up at sunrise and going to sleep content. Peace and quiet were ours. How well I recall it, how grateful I am that not all the clamour which invaded our lives later could subdue the memory or still the longing for it. Rather, it has strengthened it: had there not been what has been, I might never have known how blessed we were. (17)

The happiness recollected by Rukmani is based on an idealist's version of the simple and elemental concept of life shared by the Indian farmers for centuries.

Rukmani's disappointment at the birth of a girl child is a typical concern of an Indian farmer who needs manpower for reaping and harvesting. Her consultations with Dr. Kenny whose treatment helped her to conceive after five long years of the birth of her daughter Ira, was kept a secret to Nathan, and this act of secret treatment displays Rukmani's cleverness as well as her faith in modern science. The happiness of the agrarian couple for being blessed with sons is best revealed through her joyous reactions. Marriage of their daughter was another occasion of joy. As per the social system, even a tenant farmer had to collect dowry for marrying his daughter off. Rukmani also married her daughter, having drained the meagre store of corns she had saved for hard times. As a result the entire family had to starve when the corns failed that year, due to the cruelty of nature:

> If rained so hard, so long and so incessantly that the thought of a period of no rain provoked a mild wonder [...] the water pitilessly found every hole in the thatched roof to come in, dripping on the already damped floor [...] the waters rose and rose and the tender green of the paddy field sank under and was lost. (39)

The village dealer Biswas's inhuman treatment and greed offer a realistic picture of rural India during the last phase of the colonial rule. The greedy dealer demanded an unimaginable high price for rice he had hoarded and the tenant farmers had to lose whatever they had for a handful of rice. The cruelty of nature, either in the form of flood or of drought, was the grimmest threat to the Indian peasants, and the greed of the hoarders aggravated the situation. Moreover, there was the unrelenting landlords who demanded the rent from the tenant farmer not considering whether it was drought or flood or whether the tenant could produce any thing at all:[4]

> Harvesting time, and nothing to reap. The paddy had taken all our labour and lay now before us in faded useless heaps.
>
> Sivaji came to collect his master's dues [...]
>
> "There is nothing this year," Nathan said to him [...].
>
> "You have had the land," Sivaji said, "for which you have contracted to pay. So much money, so much rice. These are just dues. I must have them. Would you have me return empty handed?" (72-73)

At last the farmer couple had to sell all their belongings—the utensils including two brass vessels, the tin trunk and some saris used at the time of marriage, and could hardly collect half of the landlord's dues. And yet dues had to be paid, to keep the land for cultivating during the next season. It was the hope for a good rain and good crop that keeps up the farmer's stamina:

> Hope and fear. Twin forces that tugged at us first in one direction and then in another and which was the stronger no one could say. Of the latter we never spoke, but it was always with us. Fear, constant companion of the peasant. Hunger, ever at hand to jog his elbow should be relax. Despair, ready to engulf him should he falter. Fear; fear of the dark future, fear of the sharpness of hunger, fear of the blackness of death. (79)

It is the hope that ultimately wins and sustains the hungry lot. The entire texture of *Nectar in a Sieve* is woven out of fear and hope.

Cultivation is a way of life which received a set back with the advent of industrialisation. The clash between agriculture and industry is introduced in the novel through the setting up of a government tannery in the village. While some of the villagers were ready to accept the new trends of industrialization, Rukmani opposed them vehemently:

> "Never, never," I cried "They (The owners of the tannery) may live in our midst but I can never accept them, for they lay their hands upon us and we are all turned from tilling to barter, and hoard our silver since we cannot spend it, and see our children go without the food that their children gorge, and it is only in the hope that one day things will be as they were, that we have done these things. (28)

Kunthi, Kali, Janaki, the neighbours of Rukmani, "were reconciled and threw the past away with both hands that they might be the readier to grasp the present" (29), and Rukmani alone stood in pain. She, too, was reconciled when her two sons, Arjuna and Thambi, joined the tannery. She had to realise the hard fact that the land was not enough to accommodate all her sons. The growth of industrialization has been rendered through Rukmani's version:

> It was a great sprawling growth, this tannery. It grew and flourished and spread. Not a month went by but somebody's land was swallowed up, another building appeared. Night and day the tanning went on. A never ending line of carts brought the raw material in [...]. The officials of the Tannery had increased as well. Apart from the white man we had first seen—who owned the tannery and lived by himself—there were some nine or ten Muslim under him. They formed a little colony of their own [...] they were a queer lot, and their way of life was quite different from ours. (47)

Rukmani's intuitive perception came to be true as the tannery became the symbol of immorality and exploitation. Her daughter Ira who had been returned by her husband for being unable to bear a child for him, took to prostitution in the tannery colony in her despicable attempt to save her child brother Kuti from starvation. Arjun and Thamby who had joined the tannery as labourers, were dismissed by the authority as they demanded more wages. And her fourth son Raja was brutally killed by the tannery's watchman, allegedly for crossing the boundary wall and stealing one calf skin. Two persons on behalf of the authority came to Rukmini to ensure that Rukmani and Nathan should not demand any compensation for Raja's death. Rukmani had no idea that death could be compensated. The contrast between the immoral world represented by the tannery and the simple world of the peasants, comes up in the following conversation:

> 'Compensation,' I thought, what compensation is there for death? I felt confused, I did not understand what he was getting at [...].
>
> "The point is," the other said, and he thumped on the floor to emphasise his point, "that no fault attaches to us. Absolutely none [...] it is your loss, but not our responsibility [...]. (91-92)

The greed, shrewdness and inhumanity of the industrialists are revealed ironically. As Ramesh K. Srivastava rightly observed, "The tannery represents a world of immorality, greed and corruption invading another which is moral, happy and pure."[5]

The last blow from the tannery came to Rukmani when the land Nathan had taken on rent from the landlord was required for a further extension of the Tannery and Rukmani's apprehension that the tannery would eventually be their undoing, comes to be true:

> I had known it since the day the carts had come with their loads of bricks and noisy dusty men, staining the clear soft greens that had once coloured our village and cleaving its cool silences with clamour. Since then it had spread like weeds in an untended garden, strangling whatever life grew in its way. (33-34)

For Rukmani at least, the tannery strangled all her hopes and aspirations and the memory of her simple joys almost disappeared. Her two eldest sons had already gone to Ceylon, after being sacked. Her daughter gave birth to an illegitimate son, Sukrabani, and Rukmani herself had to leave the hut which her husband had built for her with his own hands:

> This hut with all its memories was to be taken from us, for it stood on land that belonged to another. And the land itself by which we lived. (135)

Besides poverty, hunger and exploitation, dislocating is one of the motifs in *Nectar in a Sieve.* Rukmani and Nathan became part of the land that they cultivated. And when they were parted from the land, their souls got uprooted, for the self and the place are conceived as well connected. An effective identifying relationship between 'self' and 'place' has been accepted by some critics as a major feature of post-colonial literature.[6] Displacement causes a crisis of identity, and the uprooted persons suffer from this crisis. When Rukmani and Nathan go to the town and learn after a long search that their son Murugan has been absconding, they have to become stone-crushers to meet their expenses. It is their uprootedness, their loss of identity in that big city, that drive them back to their village, though they do not possess any land there. They have already tasted pangs of hunger and humiliation, but never lost their spirit. This time their drooping spirit is due to a sense of insecurity that is associated with uprootedness. Nathan's drooping spirit is replaced by his jubilant cry "we shall soon be home," when, after counting the amount saved from their meagre wages, they find that they have almost collected the fare required for going back. Nathan's hope is not, however, fulfilled due to the fever that claimed his life. The lion headed orphan boy Puli who has been attached to Nathan and Rukmani during their stay in the town temple, becomes the only companion of Rukmani when Nathan dies amidst incessant rain. Even in her utter helplessness Rukmani does not lose her faith in God and in humanity. It is her unshaken faith in God and her undaunted will power that keep her spirit up in all sorts of sufferings—hunger, rootlessness and bereavement. This attitude to life enables her to accept her fate without any protest. Rukmani and Nathan belong to the last generation of Indian peasants who were regarded as idealised persons, free from greed and intolerance. The destruction of the traditional agrarian set of values due to the advent of industrialization is thus highlighted in the novel. The novel yet, ends on a positive note which a critic calls a "note of quiet strength and resolution."[7]

Accompanied by the leper orphan boy Puli, Rukmani comes back to the village after Nathan's death. She had left her son Selvam who stayed in the village to help Dr. Kenny in establishing and running a hospital. Ira and his son also stayed with Selvam. Rukmani comes back, picking up the fragments of her life, and of course with no rich promise. She does not know what her children are upto there in the village. Yet her mind becomes filled up with bliss as she enters her native village:

> So good to be home at last, at last. The cart jolted to a standstill, I looked about me at the land and it was life to my starving spirit. I felt the earth beneath my feet and wept for happiness. The time of in-between, already a memory, coiled away like a snake within its hole. From the unfinished scaffolded building a figure emerged, came running. Selvam, my son. "Thank God," he said, "Are you all right?" and he held me. My daughter joined us [...]. "Do not worry," Selvam said, "we shall manage." (189)

The concluding paragraph of the novel quoted above reveals the optimistic ring.

Rukmani is portrayed as a heroic figure whose undaunted spirit is not crushed by the most harrowing distress that could ever be imagined. Her character has been equated to Santiago in Hemingway's *Old Man and the Sea*, Ma Joad in Steinbeck's *The Grapes of Wrath* and such other figures.[8] Markandaya's hold on historiography, as is revealed in the realistic pictures of agrarian poverty, greed of the local businessmen and the landlords, and in the apathy of the colonial rule, deserves praise. But the novel hardly demonstrates what Mulk Raj Anand called "transition from the age of faith to the age of anxiety."[9] Rukmani undergoes no such transition, but clings to the ancient religious lessons and her children just escape the traditional pattern of life and embrace a new one, without experiencing the agony of leaving the old. In Markandaya's other novels, in *The Golden Honeycomb*, for example, a spirit of resistance and a desire for liberation may be traced. British hegemony is challenged in this novel on several planes: the queen Manjula and the prostitute Mohini express strong protest against all sorts of hegemony. *Nectar in a Sieve* is lacking in these qualities. A reassessment of old values which is evident in *The Golden Honeycomb*, is not found in Rukmani's readiness to accept the grimmest condition of life. Her mental make up does not fit in with the "struggles for freedom in the transition from the age of one-man rule to participatory democracy."[10] Besides, her realities hardly extend beyond the symbols associated with the formal Dharma of the past. One such symbol is a married woman's devotion to her husband. As she says to Kenny, "A woman's place is with her husband" (108). Rukmani's opinion justifies Sudhir Kakar's observation that "a girl is regarded as a guest in her own home. Her real family is her husband's family. Whatever her future fortune is when she marries, an Indian girl knows that, in a psychological sense, she can never go home again."[11] The role models who define an Indian woman's sense of identity are Sita, Savitri and Damayanti, to name a few. Rukmani has not, however, referred to these role-models. But her strong views leave no doubt in regard to her role models:

Markandaya has failed to correlate Rukmani's love for learning—it was she who taught her children how to read and write, with the approval of her illiterate husband—and the new renaissance knowledge that demanded new symbols. Rukmani's love for learning does not raise any question in her mind in regard to the status of women in the society. Though she takes her daughter to Dr. Kenny for treatment, she does not find fault with her son-in-law who remarries. Rukmani's reaction after she learns that Nathan is the father of Kunthi's sons and that he has given Kunthi a portion of rice preserved by Rukmani, is surprising. The revelation does not affect her love and devotion towards Nathan even temporarily. However, she beats Ira taking her for Kunthi in darkness, thus showing her grudge against Kunthi. But her devotion to Nathan remains unchanged. Surprisingly, again, she eats the rice brought by Ira who has prostituted herself to support the family, even when Nathan refuses to eat that ill-earned food. An Indian mother is expected to react more vehemently. Rukmani's calm acceptance of the death of her two sons, Raja and Kuti, also reveals the writer's lack of hold on the psychology of an Indian mother, Markandaya's first hand knowledge of social customs is also missing in the description of the naming ceremony of Ira's illegitimate son. The author makes a fuss about the baby's being an albino, but hardly mentions the villagers' reactions when an illegitimate child is born.

Finally, the colonial reality has not been analysed in *Nectar in a Sieve* though the fundamental role played by the colonial presence is made clear. It is only learnt through Rukmani's version that a white man owned the tannery and he lived by himself (47). There is no attempt to highlight the white man's role in generating an immoral atmosphere in the village. Rukmani's relation to Dr. Kenny and the doctor's whereabouts are kept in the dark. Arjun's ironic comment hints at his dislike of the white man. When Arjun told that he would take the help of Kunthi's son for getting a job in the tannery, Rukmani did not like the proposal:

> I did not want to be indebted to Kunthi, or to her son [...]. "There is no need to go through him," I said

> with determination. "I will ask Kenny to help you. White men have power."
> "Indeed they have," he said bitterly, "Over men, and events, and especially over women."
> "What do you mean?" I said to him, "Speak with a plain tongue or not at all."

He looked at me obliquely with darkening eyes, but would say no more (52).

Hardly anything more is said about Kenny except his benefactions. It was Kenny who arranged a servant's job for Murugan, the third son of Rukmani, in the city and both Nathan and Rukmani are thankful to him (69). It was he, again, who supplied the starving villagers with necessary help. Kenny was not in the village during the great famine, and when he came, Rukmani went to see him with a garland. Their conversation may be quoted as an instance of a romanticised version of a relationship between a white man and a native woman:

> "A garland, is it not?"
> "Yes," I said sheepishly, "I brought it for you. You guess well."
> "Not a guess," he said gravely, "a certainty, you were not the first."
> "Well-intentioned for all that—" I was beginning hotly when he began to laugh, [...] the strangeness vanished.
> "You have been away a long time," I said, "Too long, we have missed you."
> "Why"? he said, "More trouble?"
> "We have had our troubles," I said cautiously,
> "Yet it was not only on that account we missed you. It was—" I stopped, not knowing how to finish. He would have helped us in our need with food and money and skill, yet it was something more than this that he offered us, and I could not find words for it.
> "Your presence," I said haltingly, "means a lot to us. There is a rare gentleness in you, the sweeter for its brief appearances." (107)

Rukmani learns after so many years since she has been acquainted with Kenny, that his wife has left him and his sons have been taught to forget him. Though she is apprehensive of Kenny's fault, yet she holds that his wife must have accompanied him. A conversation based on poor imagination follows, pointing at the difference between a Hindu woman's approach to marriage and that of a woman in foreign countries. But the colonial presence is hardly analysed in this conversation:

> What then if his wife cannot accompany him?
> "Cannot?" I said, "She must. A woman's place is with her husband."
> He sighed impatiently. "You simplify everything, being without understanding. Your views are so limited it is impossible to explain to you."
> "Limited, yes," I agree, "Yet not wholly without understanding.
> Our ways are not your ways." (108)

Finally, Kenny helps Selvam by offering him a job. It is learnt from Selvam that Kenny is building a hospital and Selvam has been offered the job of an assistant when it is ready. At the end of the novel Selvam and Ira are seen coming out of the unfinished hospital building. Selvam's word of assurance to his mother and Ira's words that she will soon prepare rice, suggest that they have started a new life with Kenny's support. Kenny's role as a benefactor has thus been highlighted till the end of the novel, and the white hegemony is not questioned.

In conclusion, it may be reiterated that as a study of agrarian life in colonial India, *Nectar in a Sieve* falls short of a realist's approach to colonial presence. Though the novel is praiseworthy from several aspects, the joys of the agrarian life are romanticised and the protagonist is idealised.

NOTES AND REFERENCES

1. Gayatri Chakravorty Spivak observed that the "Subaltern" cannot speak. For her the word "Subaltern" is not just synonymous with 'oppressed.' According to Spivak, every thing that has limited or no access to the cultural imperialism is subaltern. *The Post Colonial Critic Interviews, Strategies, Dialogues* (London & New York: 1990) 45-46.

2. In a review of the novel published in London's Weekly, the novel was praised for its vivid record of the poverty-stricken, heart breaking existence of the peasants of the Madras Province. It was compared with *The Good Earth.* [*Indo-Anglian Fiction : An Assessment* by P.P. Mehta, Prakash Book Dipot, Bareilly (UP), 1979, 298-99.]
3. Parameswaran, Uma, *A Study of Representative Indo-English Novelists* (New Delhi: Vikas, 1976) 89.
4. Many Indian novels and stories written in the regional languages depict the relationship between landlords and the tenant farmers. The Bengali writer Tarasankar Bandopaddhaya, for example, presented this relationship from different angles. Some landlords are portrayed as cruel, some are broadminded. Some of the tenant farmers protest, some again accept the existing norm, as Rukmani does. In Tarasankar's story "Boromaloger Math' (The field of Baramalog) Balaram is a tenant farmer who tells his landlord that a tenant farmer should not demand more from the landlord who owns the land. Kamala Markandaya concentrates on the passive suffering of the tenant farmers who were compelled to starve as the landlord insisted on taking rent in time, be it drought or deluge. The relationship between the landlord and the tenant farmer has not been focused from different angles in *Nectar in a Sieve.* The famous Oriya novelist Fakir Mohan Senapati also depicted the plight of the marginalised farmers, and the greed of the local landlord. In his novel *Chha Man Athgunth,* Mangaraj and Dildar Mian are typical greedy landlords and moneylenders who exploit the poor—Saria & Bhagia, the farmer couple in the novel—and reduce them to pennyless.
5. *Six Indian Novelists in English* (Amritsar, Guru Nanak Dev University Press, 1987) 116.
6. Ashcroft, Griffiths and Tiffen, *The Empire Writes Back.* London: Routledge, 1989, 8-9.
7. K.R. Chandrasekharan, "East and West in the Novels of Kamala Markandaya," *Critical Essays on Indian Writing in English.* Eds. Naik, Desai and Amur (Dharwar: Karnatak University Press, 1968) 73.
8. Critics have traced the qualities of a tragic hero in Rukmani, and the novel is praised for depicting the tragic height. For example, Hari Mohan Prasad says "*Nectar in a Sieve* emerges as a tragedy that exalts human dignity to a new height." *The Fictional Epic on Indian Life, A Study in Theme and Technique of Nectar in a Sieve, Perspectives On Kamala Markandaya.* Ed. Madhusudan Prasad (Ghaziabad: Vimal, 1984) 100. A.V. Krishna Rao says, "Markandaya's contribution to the Indo-Anglian fiction lies essentially in her capacity to explore these vital formation areas of individual consciousness that project the images of cultural change, and in her uncanny gift of inhabiting the shifting landscape of an outer reality with human beings whose sensibility becomes a sensitive measure of the inner reality as it responds to the stimulus of change." *The Indo-Anglian Novel and the Changing Tradition* 67.

9. 'Reflections on the Novel,' *Commonwealth Literature and Problems of Response.* Ed. C.D. Narasimhaiah (Madras: Macmillan India Ltd., 1981) 49-50.
10. *Ibid.*
11. *The Inner World: A Psychoanalytic Study of Childhood and Society in India* (New Delhi: OUP, 1992) 73.

7

AESTHETICS OF THE DANCE OF SHIVA AND IMAGERY OF KAMALA DAS

A.K. AWASTHI

Art is the expression of imagination of the mind and culture its manifestation in forms of life which being diverse as well as various gives out further images and art imitates them. Thus, both complement the other in any given environment, be it natural or social. Art correlates streams of life and culture co-ordinates between its forms. This is how reality speaks and which is reflected in the cultural ethos of a region as is truly represented in the literature of this country, which in fact has lived through more or less several cultural amalgamations as reflected from lifestyle, habits, manners, faith, belief and above all socioeconomic and sociopolitical reality. Art focuses those as moods and culture adopts them as lifestyle or value and *vice versa*. Literature as art not only recreates culture, but also imparts it a new dimension.

That art and culture make a cohesive force is well illustrated by the Indian concept of the Dance of Shiva. As a mode of expression under Shaiva Aesthetics which had been elaborated by Abhinavagupta (*Dhvanyaloka*) in the ancient times and advocated by Anand Coomaraswamy in the modern times, the Dance explains all activities. The earliest reference to the Dance is found in Bharata's *Natyashastra* (as a theory of drama), in *Yogavashistha* (as a principle of nature) and of course in the *Vedas*. By following it as a standard of critical judgment, no doubt, will help us discover elements of universal appeal in literature as herein applied to the imagery of Kamala Das. It does in no way mean that K. Das's poetry is to be compared with the Dance of Shiva. No, it is not so. The Dance is taken only as a principle of Nature that is able to explain any symbolic activity. All is Nature; all activities take place in Nature with specific meanings or implications. Varieties of actions reveal purposes (as man understands) which again is a natural phenomenon. Thus any form of expression will only explain the laws of Nature. It has nothing to do with the conventional meaning of dance. As most critical theories try to interpret the meaning of poetic sensibility with specific angles, so other aspects are left unexplored. This principle tries to address meaning, intention, purpose, thought, the gross and the subtle with equal emphasis; it acquires universal ramification.

The dance represents all rhythms of life, the release from snares of illusion and heart as the centre of the universe. In fact, it is the Dance of Nature with which is identified the Wisdom of Soul; it is taking place everywhere eternally. In the poet it takes place in his heart. It has five activities or states called *Panchkriyas*, viz., *Shristi* (creation), *Stithi* (preservation, support), *Samhar* (destruction or change followed by evolution), *Tirobhava* (diffusion of illusion or materiality), and *Anugraha* (salvation, grace or sublimity). As states these imply *vibhava, anubhava, bhava, sattvabhava,* and *prakash* respectively. In Hindu mythology their symbolic representations are Brahma, Vishnu, Rudra, Maheshwara, and Sadashiva respectively. The way leading to unified experience of the true, the good, and the beautiful passes only through these states only. Hegel and Croce explain similar states in a different way and term it intuitional activity. Discovery of truth and beauty is the first step in the direction of attaining aesthetic emotion, i.e. *Rasa* the ultimate of all activities.

Underneath all activity lies "rasa" which is known as aesthetic emotion in the context of poetic activity. The poet starts from display of aesthetic emotion and arrives at identification of it with the object. The poet gets a vision of beauty at this level. Activity goes deeper still through determinants (vibhava), consequents (anubhava), moods (bhava) and involuntary emotion (sattva bhava). Finally, it is at this last state that the poet attains identification with 'rasa' itself and then performs the glorious feat of his life but thereafter ceases all activity but mechanical for ever. It implies that aesthetic emotion (rasa) overtakes the poet's mind which dances to its tune. Poetry thus produced is Shiva's Dance. 'Rasa' does not imitate nature but does reflect nature. It is not illusion nor is it unreal. It is rather an independent state of mind that combines 'vibhav,' 'anubhav' (etc.). The rise of 'sattva bhava' implies disappearance of 'Rajas' (feeling), 'tamas' (insensibility) but the poet does not remain conscious of any limitation including that of space and time. However, different states appear to be states existing outside the mind which has to attain them gradually, but it is only 'aabhas' (appearance). In fact, the initial objects which inspire the 'rasa' recede in the background and intuitive level is attained putting the poet in a state of bliss—the state of identity within the mind among its three elements—(1) Shiva (Prakash) light; (2) shakti (Vimarsh) or uma or chamatkar, *i.e.* self-consciousness; and (3) 'vyapti' (akash) the body, *i.e.* space and time in which mind exists. Thus, the mind is a self-illuminating and independent entity. The whole mind represents the Absolute in which there is no duality. The point of identity resolves all doubts and the identity itself is not union of separate categories. It is identity-in-difference. This same is called 'Ardhanarishwara,' 'Maheshwara,' 'Ardhamatra,' 'Chamatkar' or 'rasa'-aesthetic emotion. Plotinus in the western tradition holds similar views.

Bharata has clearly defined the role of 'rasa' in making an aesthetic judgment "Kavirantargatam bhavam, bhavyan bhava ucyate (NS. 79); Trailokyasyasya sarvasya, natyam bhavanukirtanum (NS. 8); Vit Vighna pratit grahyo bhav ava rasah; Bhunjanasya adbhut bhogatmak spandavistasya" (NS. 8).

It implies that the seat of emotion lies in the heart—the identity point of light and activity (wisdom); the drama celebrates this ultimate emotion; moods are basic to emotion; when the mood attains the level of enjoyment in itself, it becomes emotion (rasa).

It follows from the above that any creative activity requires the following four conditions:

1. Evidence of aesthetic (emotion) intuition
2. Vision of beauty of true creation

3. Communicability of vision
4. Stimulation of the critic to reproduce the original

These having been fulfilled entitles that work of art as representing the Dance of Shiva. It has to be remembered here that Shiva is not a personal god; it is the universal principle. It is the dance of Nature—male-female identity principle or biological principle. At the level of the individual, man is the single unity of the soul but he is not one unit of the whole. He is rather unity in himself, quite independent and at the same time identified with the cosmos or in harmony with the world. Its deepest significance is felt when it is realised that it takes place within the heart and the self. Coomaraswamy writes, "Everywhere is God, everywhere is the heart" (92).

As Shiva dances, ego is destroyed, signifying the state where illusion and impurity of deeds are burnt away. As Shiva dances his cycle of grace to destroy all to create all to destroy all, so does the Supreme Intelligence dance in the poet's soul through the conflict of opposites to accomplish the perfect union—a union of self and matter in complete identity. The reason of Shiva's dance is his own nature; it is self-nature-born. So is poetic activity to the poet. It can be neither acquired nor taught. The essential significance of poetic activity lies in identification of the dance of nature with the wisdom of soul and which is the ultimate evolution of 'rasa' or vision of beauty.

Though the dance takes place in every soul and all objects, yet it is subject to man's sensitivity as well as sensibility of it. It is known as the external principle, *i.e.* as reflected or manifest. This principle has also withstood the test of time in terms of modern science. Fritjof Capra in his book, *The Tao of Physics* mentions the dance of particles as *cosmic dance.* He conducted the Bubble-chamber experiments involving sub-atomic matter and upheld the Dance of Shiva as a scientific principle. He writes, "The bubble-chamber photographs of interacting particles which bear testimony to the continual rhythms of creation and destruction in the universe, are visual images of the Dance of Shiva equalling those of the Indian artists in beauty and profound significance. The metaphor of the cosmic dance thus unifies ancient mythology, religious art and modern physics." Further he equated it with Shiva's dance and described it in the words of Coomaraswamy, "It is poetry but nonetheless science" (*The Tao of Physics,* London, Flemings, 1991, 272). Thus the Dance of Shiva as a theory of judgment is also vindicated by science.

The Dance of Shiva implies that the Lord of the Universe is the "Dancer who like the heat latent in firewood diffuses this power in mind and matter and makes them dance in their turn" (Anand Coomaraswamy, *The Dance of Shiva,* Bombay, Asia Publishing House, 1948). Supreme intelligence dances in the human soul through the conflict of experiences to accomplish the perfect union—a vision of the self and matter in complete harmony. It is not a dance with purpose, as it is with human beings; it is self-nature born (*swabhavajah*), so is the nature of poetic activity as well. The significance of the Dance as a standard lies in the fact that in the poetry of Kamala Das images originate through her own nature and evolve along a pattern, *i.e.* the *Panchkriyas.* Love is the central theme, the aesthetic emotion—*Rasa: shringara, its sthayin being* rati (*love*).

As imagery is the dance of wisdom of soul, it follows a perfectly consistent pattern and evolution of thought. It is a figurative expression of aesthetic emotion conveying deep sensibility, an elevated viewpoint and greater comprehension of the subject. Herein an effort will be made to explain the process as well as aspects of the Dance of Shiva as it took place in her soul. Therefore her work will be considered as one effort, *i.e.* holistically. Accordingly, Shristi (creation) is represented by such images as describe suitable atmosphere to create. She regards love or sex as fundamental to creation. *Summer in Calcutta* is the preface in which the sun image reflects the energy principle—the creative principle:

I sip the
Fire, I drink and drink
Again I am drunk
Yes, but on the gold
of suns. (Further, she describes the moment of creation)
[...] How brief the term

of devotion, how brief
your reign.

It explains the energy principle as all pervading. In other words it is consciousness. But the moment of realization is brief.

Seven of her poems are highly representative in character from the viewpoint of Panchkriyas and corresponding images of the dance posture of Shiva as is represented by the famous statue of Nataraj *viz.* the drum symbolizes creation and order; lifted hand stands for preservation principle; hand holding fire for change or destruction; planted foot for diffusion of illusion and hope for man struggling in the toils of causality; lifted foot for grant of eternal bliss.

Kamala's vision proceeds with creation of a conducive environment for gaining order in terms of achieving a permanent *bhava* (theme) of love. This is symbolized by the drum and represented by the poem *An Introduction.* 'She meets a condition (*Stithi*) in which there is neither order nor support as described in the *Dance of Eunuchs,* in which Kamala is marvellous in her technique; she is both as well as each in both, *i.e.* she tries to behave like a male though she is not one. She is a woman but without grace of fulfilment—the purpose of being a woman is forfeited. She is like a eunuch who is yet to realize the satiety of identity either as a male or female or hermaphrodite even if considered in worldly terms; otherwise on cosmic level a eunuch has to attain the level of *Ardhanarishwara.* The fire-principle therefore destroys her illusion and leads the way to make her assert as in *Composition.* She becomes brave and comes out of toils of causality, *i.e.,* the worldly tantrums (*Samhar*). The next is *Tirobhava,* when she discovers this; it is not the physical satisfaction but the mental or emotional which has value and is capable of giving satiety. Finally, stability is gained when she attains *Anugraha* in *Phantom Lotus.* The foot planted on the ground symbolizes it. It is followed by realization (symbolized by the lifted foot) that love of man, *i.e.,* any man, would not satisfy her. Anyone capable of granting her eternal bliss alone would be the embodiment of fulfilment of love and it is the love of Ghanshyam (in the poem of the same title) which would make her realize the aesthetic emotion (*Rasa*)—the moving spirit behind her poetic process.

An Introduction represents the sacred drum of Shiva that establishes order in the universe. She gains her identity as the female principle [...]:

> I was a child and later they told me I grew [...] my limbs swelled and one or two places sprouted hair
> and she (I) felt the "*weight of my breasts and womb crushed me* [...]"
>
> "I met a man, loved him, call
> Him not by any name, he is every man,
> who wants a woman, just as I am every woman,
> who seeks love
> [...] Who are you, I ask each and every one,
> the answer is, it is I."

It is in this poem that she feels the "*hungry haste of rivers in me* [...] *the oceans' tireless waiting.*" From "*the trees in storm* to *blazing funeral pyre*" to "*haste of rivers*" to '*I*' to "*it is I who laugh,*" the journey of creation is complete. All the five elements meet as inspired by the drum.

The Dance of Eunuchs is characteristic of displaying the reality both external and internal, *i.e.*, social and emotional. The eunuchs are celebrating the birth of a child making "coquettish *gestures*" and "*thumping on their little drums*" they appear "*so unwholesome and sinister that I was fascinated.*" The poem represents the Shakti principle reflecting five triangles (as per *sricakra*) or images: (1) sound, (2) rainfall and humidity, (3) passion, (4) hope for a change, (5) search for identity or fulfilment. 'The raised hand' in the dance-posture of Natraj icon represents it. It illustrates two aspects of the dance—the lifted hand of hope and the hand holding fire—which imply the urge for protection and transformation respectively. It is this underlying feeling that is communicated to the reader as the final impression. Eunuchs are guided by the self-born desire, as is the nature of Shiva Himself. Conditions of heat followed by rainfall represent humidity and vital discharge, the seminal principle to create—"*smell of dust in attics and urine of lizards and mice.*"

"*Jingling*" repeated three times indicates rhythm of dance of creation. The whirling movement and frenzy contrasted with "*inner vacuity*" represent passion which is expressed by action and desire of fulfilment, the two basics of any spherical phenomenon. She writes:

Beneath the fiery gulmohar with
Long braids flashing,
Dark eyes flashing they danced and they danced,
Oh! They danced till they bled [...].

The poet's emotional vacuity is identified with that of eunuchs.

The image of eunuchs who are neither male nor female clearly represents the *Ardhanarishwara,* i.e. Shiva, and Shakti are identified, become one comprising both the qualities just in half. Gulmohar is fiery and atmosphere hot means that the desire is intense and excitement is high. Their harsh voices are different from both—a normal male and a normal female—but their nasal sounds signify that the female elements are quite in harmony with the harsh tone of the male masculinity. Pathos as expressed by the metaphor of 'half-burnt logs from the funeral pyres' reflects a state of pause after creation. This is *Stithi,* the second state as under *Panchkriyas,* the first *Shristi* having been described above. The following lines illustrate the present condition:

some beat their drums; others their sorry breasts
And wailed and wailed in vacant ecstasy.

This is 'unfulfilment.' In reality it is no pathetic state but preservation. As *Samhara* (change) precedes creation 'the half-burnt logs' imply that energy and matter still exist and nothing is destroyed completely. Eunuchs sterility is a great principle in itself—the basic one. It represents *Shakti,* which is the principle of action and identified with Shiva. *Shakti* is passion and it is in constant search of Shiva—the principle manifest in nature—in order to gain the identity-in-difference. Use of the phrase 'vacant ecstasy' in fact, reflects the essential condition for making any effort of that kind. The funeral imagery is obviously, *Samhara* (destruction followed by evolution). It implies destruction of negative forces like want and lust. Evolution can follow only after this process. When we read

Summer in Calcutta with *Dance of Eunuchs,* an evidence is found about the use of (*panchbhuta*), air, fire, water, earth, which play their respective role in *aakash*—the fifth basic element, in the body or the universe.

The Freaks is a poem that complements *Dance of Eunuchs.* It describes human body as a cavern, a prison house of soul, which desires to satisfy not the "skin's lazy hungers" but "the heart, an empty cistern, waiting." In the state of want she fills it "with calling snakes of silence" (again implying the *Shakti* principle) and indulges in lust as meaningless activity "just to save my face."

Composition illustrates the journey from destruction of negative attitude to transformation in the form of escape from snares of illusion as symbolized by the arch of fire behind the dancing Shiva and the foot planted on the ground. The poem symbolizes Kamala's crusade to liberate her and the womankind from rotten social norms:

> Ultimately
> I have come face to face with sea

is symbolic of *bhavasagar,* the storehouse of sensory experiences. She destroys the myth of physical love as the supreme factor in life. As such love and hate are involvements. She writes: *This only signifies growth and growth is natural.*

The tragedy of life in not death but growth, implies that knowledge of the world, awareness of want or loss, pleasure or pain leads to tragedy. It is a paradox for tragedy lies in being unable to look beyond conditioning of life and death, in considering only material or physical development as symbolic of growth:

> I was busy growing.
> I Had then no time at all for the sea
> There was off and on a seascape.

For the freedom, her husband gave her, made her only a 'plain frigid.' Now worldly definitions of love and friendship do not interest her any more:

> I must let my mind striptease
> I must extrude autobiography.

Further,

> Only those who like to listen, listen
> To the deeply felt vibrations of the heart

and

> By peeling off my layers
> I reach closer to the soul.

Now she is free and also morally strong enough to recreate a new society to present the truth threadbare:

> Ultimately
> I will feed only the hunger
> To feed other hungers
> That basic one
> To crumble
> To dissolve
> And to retain in other things
> The potent fragments
> Of myself, my only freedom being
> The freedom
> To discompose.

Composition is perhaps the only poem in which all the four levels of *Panchkriyas* that take place in her mind are well reflected and journey to the fifth begins. On reading this poem with *Suicide,* the point is well proved.

Phantom Lotus represents the fourth level of activity (*Tirobhava*)—the image of the foot aloft of the dancing Shiva. It gives a perfect picture of release. Now she no longer needs to 'save her face' 'to flaunt at flamboyant lust' for she has learnt to be simple (as in *Suicide: I want to be simple, I want to be loved*); she has realized instead:

> The only truth that matters
> That all this love is mine to give
> [...] Heed my faith alone [...]
> I seek but another way to know
> Him who has no more a body
> To offer and whose blue face is
> A Phantom Lotus on the waters of my dreams.

Such evolution is also illustrated in other poems like The

Blind Walk, The Lion; A Man is a Season; Morning At Apollo Pier; Sunset, Blue Bird; Lines Addressed to a Devdasi; etc.

Finally, the fifth activity (*Anugraha*) sets in. It is represented by Shiva's hand pointing towards the lifted foot, that grants eternal bliss, the last refuge of the soul—the merger, the unity, the identity, whatever name we give to that state, but that is the ultimate for any poet when he/she gains sublimity. For Kamala Das this is an evolution from sensual love to realization of esthetic emotion, love of soul, illustrating an intuitive approach to life. *Ghanshyam* and *Radha* are the poems that are devoted to the principle of love, the poet's ultimate:

> Ghanshyam
> You have like a koel built your
> Nest in the arbour of my heart
> My life until now a sleeping jungle [...]
> If *he* is you and I am you
> Who is loving who
> Who is the husk who the kernel
> Where is the body where is the soul [...].

Herein the very duality disappears. As the experience of *Satcidanand* (supreme bliss) cannot be expressed in words, so she says:

> Wisdom must come in silence [...]
> Steal in like a breeze [...]
> And towards you my thoughts today
> Must race like enchanted fish [...].

Anugraha (salvation, grace or sublimity) signifying realization of truth or social reality reaches the full mark. She begins with *the long waiting and reasoning follows* [...]. *Then a virgin cries for love* [...] and she finds:

> Everything in me
> Is melting even the hardness at the core of Krishna.
> I am melting, melting;
> Nothing remains but you.

This is pure bliss, eternal peace, silence, and eternal light.

In *A Request,* Kamala gives a befitting finish to her evolving poetic process. Now, she has gained humility:

When I die,
Do not throw
The meat and bones away,
But pile them up.
And let them tell
By their smell,
What life was worth
On this earth;
What love was worth
In the *end*.

Thus imagery in the poetry of Kamala Das faithfully illustrates the dance of Nature and wisdom of Soul, known as the Dance of Shiva. She does not simply gain unity with the cosmic soul rather she arrives at identity-in-difference, for only ONE remains.

It is only through such prophetic evolution of soul that she destroys the stigma attached to (her) sex-talk, and exposes selfish attitude of man and openly seeks refuge in an all-embracing love of Krishna, who is the embodiment of love. She establishes that God is love and love God. Kamala has proved that she has transcended the three dimensional unity of the subject, which is bound by space-time relativity, therefore she conceives beyond it and tries to impart sublime effect to poetry much in the same way in what Coleridge refers to the role of imagination as the shaping and modifying power and capable of gaining objectivity, in which the person of the poet merges with the Cosmic I. Her wisdom has danced to the tune of cosmic intelligence while communicating her experience only objectively or in other words, in subjectivity-abnegation objectified manner. The two worlds of spirit and matter (or *purush and prakriti*) have become-one through her imagery.

Kamala Das is one of the bravest and most positive of Indian writers of English. Perhaps she is better than most other poets, whose words are refined, no doubt, but their minds are prisoners of socio-moral conditioning. They have never realized the truth, nor have they stood before their own conscience to reassure themselves about discharging their socio-moral as well as artistic responsibility. Kamala

Das on the contrary became a movement in herself, launched a crusade to destroy illusion through symbols which were considered immoral (in fact, sex is the seminal principle of life and the Dance of Shiva incorporates it) and thus provided an inspiration to the post-generation. She remains the symbol of *Prakriti* (eternal Nature) and her imagery its dance. Her decisions regarding personal life also vindicate the same.

BIBLIOGRAPHY

Das, Kamala. *Summer in Calcutta.* New Delhi: Everest Press, 1965.

——. *The Descendants.* Calcutta: Writer's Workshop, 1965.

——. *The Old Play House and Other Poems.* Madras: Orient Longman, 1973.

——. *The Love Poems of Kamala Das and Pritish Nandi.* New Delhi: Arnold Heinemann, 1979.

——. *Collected Poems.* Trivandrum, 1984.

Capra, Fritjof. *The Tao of Physics.* London: Flemings, 1991.

Coomaraswamy, Anand K. *The Dance of Shiva.* Bombay: Asia Publishing House, 1948.

——. *Yogavasishtha.* Gorakhpur: Gita Press, 1968.

——. *Natyashastra.*

8

SAHGAL'S FEMALE PROTAGONISTS: *STORM IN CHANDIGARH* AND *THE DAY IN SHADOW*

BEULAH RANJITSINGH

The roles the Indian women play have undergone dramatic changes from one era to another, varying from caste to caste and milieu to milieu. Indian women in the Vedic age enjoyed a comparatively higher status than that was enjoyed by their sisters in the post Vedic age. They were educated and treated not only with grace but also with courtesy and consideration. They enjoyed almost an equal status with men in the family, the society and the state. The status of women in India began to decline around 300 BC, as the education of women received a set back from then onwards with the introduction of child-marriage. There was a slow but steady eclipse in the status accorded to women both at home and in society. With Manu, the law-giver of the Hindus, advocating a male-centred and male-dominating society, a gradual deterioration in the status of women occurred in the post Vedic period. The epics and the poems of this time extol women for their subservience and faithfulness. Sita, the silent sufferer of the epic *Ramayana*, became the archetype of Indian womanhood with all her self-effacing wifely qualities of loyalty, submission and chastity. In the nineteenth and early twentieth centuries women occupied a very low status in Indian society. A woman confined to the home often lived the life of a domestic servant or was merely a child-bearer to her husband. The continuing trend of exploitation of woman by man provokes her to revolt against the social system. The rapid strides in higher education made the women self-reliant. The awareness of the need for liberation from the shackles of marital bondage has been felt by many an educated woman in the post-Independence era.

The theme of modern woman's existential struggle to establish her own identity in order to assert her individuality surfaces quite often in the novels of the Indian women novelists of the post-Independence age as can be seen in the works of Kamala Markandaya, Ruth Prawer Jhabvala, Anita Desai and Nayantara Sahgal. As a novelist, Kamala Markandaya is intensely aware of the impact of the socio-economic forces on contemporary women. In her novel *Nectar in a Sieve* Rukmani, the protagonist, is presented as a 'woman of sorrows' barely managing to survive in a south Indian village. Ruth Prawer Jhabvala's novel *Get Ready for Battle* presents the bitter survival of Sarala Devi, a middle aged woman fretting under her oppressive, materialistic husband Gulzarilal who is counting on nothing but his wealth and her obedience. The existential plight of women in a male-dominated society is effectively presented in Anita Desai's fiction too. Her women characters are in perpetual quest for some meaning or value in life. Maya in her novel *Cry, the Peacock* inhabits a world full of morbid fears and turns neurotic and eventually psychotic, because of her failure to establish a cordial and satisfactory relationship with her husband Gautama. Having experienced the bitterness and agony of marital discord which ultimately resulted in a divorce in her own life, Nayantara Sahgal depicts in her novels an Indian woman's struggle for survival in the present-day world and her quest for individual freedom and self-identity. With a profound understanding of feminine sensibility, she explores and voices the mute miseries of millions of married women through her works of fiction.

Nayantara Sahgal presents in her novels the emergence of the 'new woman' who is no longer "a sex object and glamour girl, fed on fake dreams of perpetual youth, lulled into passive role that requires no individuality" (Sahgal 19 July 1970), but someone who can claim to be man's equal and honoured partner. Different types of couples are presented in her novels who live behind a façade apparently basking in hypocritical terms of endearment and gestures of love in marriage. Several married women in her fictional world undergo moments of excruciating mental torture within themselves. In her early novels Mrs Sahgal presents devoted, loyal and tradition-bound wives who patiently put up with everything in marriage and do not think of quitting the family structure as they are hamstrung in the fabric of Indian culture. However, Mrs Sahgal gradually begins to deal with problems of women who are not satisfied with their marital relationships in her later novels. If the women are utterly submissive and traditional in her first two novels namely *A Time to be Happy* and *This Time of Morning*, her next two novels *Storm in Chandigarh* and *The Day in Shadow* present women as more progressive and rebellious.

Of Mrs Sahgal's eight novels, this paper confines its scope of discussion selectively to two novels namely *Storm in Chandigarh* and *The Day in Shadow* as these novels present very authentically and specifically the sad plight of women in the male-dominated society. The female protagonists of these novels experience conflict, frustration, longdrawn period of stress and bitterness in the prison house of loveless marriage. The novels also show how the protagonists mature through their bitter experiences and eventually find a stable identity of their own.

Saroj, the female protagonist, in *Storm in Chandigarh* falls a prey to the suspicion and anger of her husband Inder as she innocently confesses to him on one occasion that "she just out of college, the ink hardly dry on her fingers, history and literature fresh on her tongue" and "enchantingly innocent" (96) had an affair with a young boy. From that very moment Saroj becomes a frequent victim and a permanent object of suspicion in the eyes of her husband Inder who is not able to forgive his wife's innocent pre-marital affair. It is quite ironical that Inder considers it to be a serious moral lapse in Saroj, his wife while he himself carries on an extra-marital affair with his children's teacher Mara. The society which lives by a double moral standard one for men and other for women brands her guilty. Inder feels that he has been cheated and Saroj's act cannot be justified:

> It had no place in an order that clearly demarcated the roles of men and women, unless that venerable order was breached, trampled and mocked. He was maddened

> by it. When it came over him he sat looking at Saroj with a revulsion that had ancient, tribal, male roots. (*Storm in Chandigarh* 96)

Even after four years of married life and having two children, Inder continues to develop a deep seated doubt about Saroj's loyalty and brutally pesters her with persistent questions on her pre-marital affair:

> "A friend? To go to bed with? How many times did it happen?"
>
> "I don't know. I can't remember"
>
> [...] For each time she had lived through a night's torment.
>
> [...] "How many times?" He repeated in the flat, taut monotone of illness.
>
> "Four, five. It was so long ago. I'm not sure."
>
> "You're not sure." The voice, remote and dangerous, unpredicable as a rawhide whip, flicked at her nerves. (94)

Once when they as a family are on a picnic, all on a sudden Inder starts questioning Saroj about her past:

> "Well, why did you do it? That is what I keep coming back to?
>
> Why did you do it?"
>
> "I was fond of him," she said wearily, "and I was curious. Is that a crime?"
>
> "Good God [...]. Wouldn't your curiosity wait till you got married?" (129)

Inder can love Saroj only in the capacity of an obedient slave, a possession or commodity. He can never think of her as a person with ideas, feelings and emotions. To Inder a Business man "A wife was one half an enterprise, the compliant partner, who presided over home and children and furthered her husband's career" (53). Inder is unable to view any other kind of relationship other than this with Saroj. M.L. Malhotra rightly points out the male-chauvinism in Inder thus:

> Belong as he does to the he-man school and born and brought up as he is in an atmosphere, where male-dominance is a formidable cult, there is no question of

any freedom or self-expression or growth for Saroj, nor of any mutual co-partnership between them. (1971, 230)

Saroj willingly accepts her role as a wife to Inder and tries her best to adjust compromise and strengthen her relationship with Inder but in vain. She has been living in the house entirely on Inder's terms. Yet she finds no happiness or satisfaction in her conjugal relationship. She has to strive hard to build a working relationship with her husband who bars her entry into his world. She does not feel free to express her thoughts and she is all the time afraid "of saying the wrong thing or of being misunderstood—Just of being oneself and being punished for it" (89). She feels alienated and expresses with deep anguish and distress, "I am alone even when Inder is here" (223). She boldly puts up with Inder's idiosyncrasies for the sake of her two children and as she is expecting her third child, she finds it very difficult to keep on living with her husband under the same roof with no real bond between them.

In course of time, the gulf gradually becomes wider and wider in Saroj-lnder relationship as he has no time for emotional involvement and shows a lot of indifference towards her. He considers taking his wife on a walk in the pleasant evenings "a meaningless expenditure of time, when a restlessness took hold of him to get back to whatever work he had to do" (53). Saroj who longs for "the oxygen of understanding" (220) finds it in her friendship with Vishal Dubey who has come as liaison officer to Chandigarh to settle the political problem between the Chief Ministers of Punjab and Haryana and develops a cordial relationship with him. Being attracted by Saroj's childlike innocence, Dubey draws himself emotionally close to her.

Going on long walks with Dubey, Saroj feels relieved and freshened from the suffocation of the four walls of her home. Saroj who has been so long in dire need for 'someone to talk to' (201) finds in Dubey a comforting reciprocative companion. The frequent visits of Dubey to their house and Saroj going on long walks with him enrage the envious and suspicious husband Inder and he objects her act. Inder gets irritated about Saroj's absence from home and snubs her. Saroj's bold reply "I like to talk to him, [...]. He's a good man" (193) infuriates Inder who thrashes her not only with words but also with blows. During their long walks in the jungle, Dubey instills in Saroj the value of emancipation and the courage to defy Inder. So Saroj turns a deaf ear to all her husband's frantic admonitions. In the end, she emerges with a new found courage and plans to go with her children to New Delhi for her confinement at the suggestion of Dubey. By moving out of Inder's house, she moves out of the virtuous stereotype which consigns a woman to perpetual humiliation and denies her self-expression. Lakshmi Sinha comments on Saroj's act of leaving Inder in these words: "Saroj leaves domesticity and timidness far behind and emerges out of her chrysalis with a new found confidence. Dubey has resurrected her personality and at no cost is he going to let it collapse again" (1987, 109). Saroj leaves Inder apparently to start life afresh with Dubey who understands her delicate sentiments and emotional needs.

If Saroj's marriage fails due to lack of understanding and communion Simrit in the sequel novel *The Day in Shadow* fails to build up a satisfactory marital relationship with her husband Som because of her own temperamental disparity with him. According to Jasbir Jain, "Simrit's story in *The Day in Shadow* is in many ways the continuation of Saroj's" (1994, 40). The novel narrates the story of Som and Simrit who seem to get on well during the first few years of their marriage. But soon he fails to comprehend the sensibilities of Simrit. He treats her not as a person but as a possession. Mrs Sahgal regards Som as a typical chauvinistic representative of "ruthless, self-centred anglicized business tycoons, belonging to the he-man school, whose male-dominance is the most formidable cult" (12 Dec. 1971). In the earlier novel Saroj actively contemplates divorce whereas in *The Day in Shadow* Simrit actually divorces her husband at the risk of facing misery, economic constraints, depressive bouts of loneliness and a score of other existential problems. In a flash back Simrit's discontented and bitter life in a male-dominated society is presented in the novel.

Just like Saroj, Simrit also finds herself utterly shut out of the world of her husband who never discusses business with her or in her presence. Ironically, Simrit realizes that verbal communication is the missing link in her relationship with Som and tries in vain to engage him in some meaningful dialogue or other. Som pays no heed to Simrit's words even in making ordinary decisions of everday life. Simrit cannot purchase or even change chair covers and curtains without Som's permission. If she punished the cook and dismissed him for "drunkenness and bad behaviour" (*The Day in Shadow* 38), Som retained him. "Not even about chair covers and curtains. Even there Som had had a veto. Not even about servants" (38). Instead, Som treats her merely as a sexual object. But for her, emotional involvement is far more important than sexual relationship. Som's finalisation of a new deal of armament depresses Simrit further. While Simrit feels sad thinking of the disaster connected with the armament he has entered into, he revels on the prospect of his prosperity. For Som self-advancement is the only goal in life. It is the clash of ideals that leads to their separation. Simrit finds herself unable to respond to her husband's physical needs and remains "separate, excluded, rebellious" (90). Som who feels insulted at Simrit's physical withdrawal, reacts wildly and walks out of her life. Greatly upset, Simrit is left with no other option than divorce. Eventually what forces Simrit to rebel against her bond of marriage is "her yearning for a free communication of ideas with her husband, beyond the glandular sensation of sex" (Rao: 1976, 58). On obtaining her divorce, she settles down to a life with her children in her newly rented flat in the Defence Colony. The desperate Simrit does not grumble about her responsibility of looking after her children in this situation.

For Simrit divorce does not bring freedom but confrontation with all that is orthodox in "this man-centred society. Som imposes cruel divorce terms on Simrit in revenge. Even after divorce Som in order to save his own income tax, thrusts cruel consent terms on Simrit, according to which she has to pay "huge taxes" (55) on the shares worth six lakhs which are presently in her name but will go to her son Brij, aged sixteen when he attains the age of twenty-five. Simrit's efforts to get rid of these unfair, unjudicious terms fail. She pleads with Som's lawyer: "I don't want the shares left in my name. As long as they are, I'll have to pay this crippling tax and whatever

I earn will just be wiped out by the tax" (56). The huge tax makes her utterly devastated and overwhelmed. She feels reduced almost to the level of a beast of burden:

> [...] this is what an overloaded donkey feels like standing there as large as life with its back breaking, and no one doing anything about it, not because they can't see it, but because it's a donkey and loads are for donkeys. (56)

Simrit feels utterly lost and bewildered at the brutal divorce settlement inflicted upon her. She feels uprooted and abandoned as divorce is considered as scandalous and stigmatic in the Indian society which refuses to recognise a woman's identity apart from that of her husband. Simrit is curiously looked down by others "as if divorce were a disease that left pock marks" (4). Being a free-lance journalist and writer she feels relatively at home only in intellectual circles and parties such as those constituted by journalists just like herself. Struggling to build a new life for herself and her children, she encounters Raj Garg, a brilliant rising Member of Parliament. Eventually, she seeks Raj's help to get out of the legal morass created by her divorce settlement. Raj who understands and shares her agony instills in her some positive thinking to face the world with renewed confidence in herself. He tells her, "It's time to cut loose all those ragged ends, all the bleeding bits of the past, and get on with your life" (39). Raj's broad sympathies and humane attitude draw Simrit towards him and she decides to marry him. Raj-Simrit relationship, according to Shyam, M. Asnani is "grounded in sympathy and empathy, rather than bestial sensuality and cruel insensitivity" (1985, 130).

The two novels *Storm in Chandigarh* and *The Day in Shadow* discussed in this paper can be grouped together not only from the thematic point of view but also from the point of view of the sustained moral vision of the novelist that shapes and directs the destinies of the female protagonists. These two novels are very authentic in dealing with the theme of women's suppression and revolt in the socio-political set up in modern India as the protagonists' struggle for freedom is derived directly from the novelist's personal experience. The female protagonist Saroj's bitter experience of falling a prey to the suspicion and anger of her husband Inder springs out from Mrs Sahgal's own personal experience. The novelist mentioning about her pre-marital affair to her husband had sown seeds of suspicion and jealousy in Gautam, her husband and it resulted in a storm in her domestic life. Inder's reactions to Saroj's pre-marital love affair are nothing but a vivid recall of Gautam's callousness. Mrs Sahgal was tormented with pestering questions on her past-affair, suspected and denied self-expression. She found friendship outside marriage quite satisfactory and spent long hours with Kjeld, a German friend. Gautam became more suspicious and attempted to discourage Nayantara moving with other men. With the personal experience of the trauma she underwent in her married life under the watchful eyes of her husband, the novelist brings out vividly the bitter struggle for survival of Saroj with the suspicious husband Inder.

Simrit in *The Day in Shadow* bears in many respects, the image of her author. The agony of Simrit as a divorcee seems to find some authentic echoes from Mrs Sahgal's personal life as it was written in 1970 soon after her own divorce in 1967. The novelist herself acknowledges the above fact in her article "Of Divorce and Hindu Woman." Referring to *The Day in Shadow* she observes:

> In this book I tried to figure out something that has happened to me—the shattering experience of divorce. I wanted to show how even in a free country like ours, where women are equal citizens, a woman can be criminally exploited without creating a ripple. (12 Dec. 1971)

Like her creator, Simrit is a free-lance journalist and writer who gets married to a businessman of her own choice and experiences a sense of bewilderment and a shattering emotional shock of her divorce and the brutal consequences of an unfair divorce settlement, inflicted on her after seventeen years of married life. Mrs Sahgal felt over burdened with the enormity of her tax burden thrust upon her by the divorce settlement. Eventually, she overcame her problem of tax only through her own independent efforts. In her interview to Jasbir Jain she says:

> My husband defrauded me also. Not only defrauded me but hung me with taxes. I would not have had otherwise. I had a huge struggle after the divorce to make money and I made it. I feel pleased that I managed to do it [...] by my own efforts. (1994, 185)

Having experienced in her own life the bitterness of the exploitation of woman and denial of justice to her by man and society, Mrs Sahgal presents through the protagonist Simrit the existential problems of women in a male-dominated society in a realistic manner. Mrs Sahgal after having been abandoned by her husband found a true companion in a Christian Government official E.N. Mangat Rai I.C.S. and got married to him. In the novel she makes her protagonist Simrit too find, after her divorce, comfort and comradeship in the company of a Christian Member of Parliament Raj Garg whom she decides to marry. The autobiographical elements are more predominant in these two novels under discussion than in any of Mrs Sahgal's fictional work.

It is significant to note that just like their creator, both Saroj and Simrit try their best to be good wives as long as their marriages last and never take the conventional family structure lightly. It is only circumstances beyond their control that make them quit their respective households. Both of them stand for the emerging women of India who refuse to remain silent and submissive like conventional 'pativratas' in marriage. Breaking the shackles of hapless marriage, they prefer to live a life with their lovers who can provide them with understanding, love and warmth of companionship and help them start life afresh. Neena Arora observes:

> Sahgal's women depend on some help to escape oppression and exploitation which in their cases is usually provided by a man—a friend or a father—who often helps them to come out of the miserable relationship or give them moral strength to smash the taboos and assert their identity to live a meaningful life. (1991, 102)

Nayantara Sahgal is not opposed to marriage as a social institution but stresses the greater need for loyalty and mutual understanding in any lasting man-woman relationship. Chaman

Nahal commenting upon Mrs Sahgal's novels points out: "In each case the attack is not against the institution of marriage but against the inequality and injustice that is forced upon women by men using the institution of marriage" (1985, 102).

Alienation, resulting from lack of communication and mutual infidelity, forms the 'stoff' of *Storm in Chandigarh* whereas *The Day in Shadow* shows how lack of understanding and inability to strike a sympathetic chord in marital relationship ultimately lead to divorce. The female protagonists of both the novels are striving hard for constructive and meaningful relationship with their men demanding mutual understanding and involvement. Having failed in their attempts, as liberated women they flee from their bitter survival to better survival. Thus Nayantara Sahgal's women as she herself acknowledges, are "strivers and aspirers towards freedom, towards goodness, towards a compassionate world" (qtd. in Jain: 1994, 116).

WORKS CITED

Arora, Neena. *Nayantara Sahgal and Doris Lessing: A Feminist Study in Comparison.* New Delhi: Prestige Books, 1991.

Asnani, Shyam, M. *Critical Response to Indo English Fiction.* Delhi: Mittal Publications, 1985.

Jain, Jasbir. *Nayantara Sahgal.* Rev. ed. Jaipur: Printwell, 1994.

Malhotra, M.L. *Bridges of Literature.* Ajmer: Sunanda Publications, 1971.

Nahal, Chaman. *The New Literatures in English.* New Delhi : Allied Pulbishers Pvt. Ltd., 1985.

Rao, A.V. Krishna. *Nayantara Sahgal: A Study of Her Fiction and Non-Fiction.* Madras: M. Seshachalam & Co., 1976.

Sahgal, Nayantara. *Storm in Chandigarh.* Delhi: Hind Pocket Books (P) Ltd., 1970.

——. *The Day in Shadow.* New Delhi: Penguin Books India (P) Ltd., 1971.

——. "Of Divorce and Hindu Woman." *The Hindustan Times* 12 December 1971.

——. "Women: Persons or Possessions." *The Hindustan Times* 19 July 1970.

Sinha, Lakshmi. "Nayantara Sahgal *Storm in Chandigarh*: A Search for Values." *Studies in Indian Fiction in English.* Ed. G.S. Balarama Gupta. Gulbarga: JIWE Publications, 1987. 104-12.

9

MAN-WOMAN RELATION IN THE NOVELS OF ANITA DESAI

AJAY K. GHOSH

Complex human relation, particularly that of man and woman may be considered as the major theme regularly and recurringly used by Anita Desai in her novels to dramatically picture the psychological development and inward reality of her characters. The theme has been as old as the novel itself and can be found in Richardson and Fielding on the one hand and D.H. Lawrence, Virginia Woolf, Hemingway and Faulkner on the other. The relation between man and woman has become more important for industrial revolution, which is responsible for rapid industrialization, growth of consciousness among women about their rights and individualities and also the Westernization of attitudes and lives of people. The Indian English novelists R.K. Narayan in *The Dark Room* and *The Guide,* Raja Rao in *The Serpent and the Rope,* Mulk Raj Anand in *Gauri,* Bhabani Bhattacharyya in *Music for Mohini,* Manohar Malgonkar in *A Bend in the Ganges* and Arun Joshi in *The Foreigner* and *The Strange Case of Billy Biswas* discuss the incompatible man-woman relation in the novels. What Mrs Desai does in her treatment in this theme is that she explores the psychological depth of her characters very minutely and analyses their motives extremely thoroughly. The earlier Indian English novelists did not attempt such acute analysis. To Mrs Desai fluctuating relation between man and woman is more important than the plot or story of a novel. Let us discuss her novels one by one.

In her first novel *Cry, the Peacock,* the dreamy and demented wife Maya and her practical lawyer husband

Gautama have strained relation because of their incompatible temperaments. Maya is sensitive and emotional while Gautama is insensitive and rational; Maya is fanciful while Gautama is realistic; one is emotional and high-strung; the other is detached, philosophical, remote. Maya is soft and warm; Gautama is hard and cold. The wife is the creature of instinct; the husband is that of intellect. To Gautama love is merely an attachment. It is scanty and meagre. He is 'too fastidious to admit such matters as love, with its accompanying horror of copulation, of physical demands and even, overbearingly, spiritual demands of possession and rights won and established' (113). But 'passion, revenge, murder or exciting things' (20) like love, life or death of Toto are basic and important things to her. Thus the matrimonial bonds that bind the two are very fragile and tenuous 'neither true nor lasting' but 'broken repeatedly' (40).

The astrologer's prophesy 'death to one of you' (30) prompts Maya to mobilize her urgency to enjoy life with Gautama but in 'the distance he coldly keeps from' (9) her, she hears the love-tortured peacocks' death bearing cry 'lover, I die' (97). The images of birds like mating doves and animals like neck-tied bear and caged monkey suggest Maya's suffering due to the distancc and strained relation between the two. From Gautam's theory of detachment and father's acceptance she turns to her friends, Lila and Pom who dishearten her, widen the distance between the two and darken their emotional vacuum which is filled with gloom and misery. The growing tension due to lack of communication and sweet emotional bond reaches its climax when mentally unbalanced Maya considers the cold lifeless and unresponsive Gautama unfit for life and without any qualms of conscience kills him by pushing him from the roof down to the earth. Later, a victim of emotional gloom and existential anguish, she commits suicide.

In *Voices in the City* the theme of man-woman relation is treated in a somewhat different way. The theme is juxtaposed in the plot mainly in triple ways—the illegal relation between Nirode's mother and Major Chadha, the strained relation between Jiban, Nirode's brother-in-law and Monisha, his elder sister and also the strained relation between Dharma, the mysterious artist and Amla, Nirode's youngest sister. In the first case the seed of Nirode's alienation is sown. Nirode is upset over his mother's clandestine affair with Major Chadha. The letters that Nirode's mother gave him show her shameless relation with the Punjabi gentleman who entered their house and finally seduced her. Nirode is at loggerheads with his mother and refuses to take her money even at the time of his bare need and tells Monisha: 'Tell her to shove it up that old Major of hers, all her stinking cheques' (134). Though Nirode hates his mother, he has respect for his father who was a lazy, relaxing type of person. In fact Nirode's mother had a terrible contempt for and resentment about her lazy husband. So the relation between Nirode's father and mother was far from satisfactory.

The ideal and mysterious love that grew between Amla and Dharna again shows the strained relation between the two. The sudden meeting between Amla and Dharma in his house roused secret love in Amla for Dharma, the silent and mysterious artist of Calcutta living away from the city in the cool lap of nature. Dharma was also attracted by Amla's physical features and asked her to serve as his model. Amla was touched as well as frustrated by love. She realized that 'she was overflowing with a sense of love' (210), but also realized that Dharma was unable to offer her 'tangibility, permanence' (212). Gradually Amla learns that in her Dharma rediscovered his long-lost rebellious daughter Mrinalini who eloped with her first cousin. Thus the relation between Dharma and Amla which was based on love, sympathy and understanding came to nothing leaving passion-tortured Amla utterly frustrated. The most remarkable example of strained relation between man and woman in the novel is the incompatible marriage of Jiban and Monisha. Jiban, the husband of Monisha is a rational diplomat living in Calcutta, who cannot reach to the emotional world of his wife, Monisha. Monisha, being an educated woman of unconventional outlook cannot adjust with the conventional family of Jiban at Bahubazar in the monotonously buzzing city of Calcutta. Moreover the knowledge that her womb is unfertile to produce any child, makes the family apathetic and negligent towards her and Jiban's charge of theft 'why did not you tell me before you took it?' (138) in course of his acknowledgment that it is Monisha who had taken his money without obtaining his prior permission to pay Nirode's hospital bill suggests the strained and unhappy relation between the two. Monisha thought that she had every right to Jiban's money, so she took it without his prior permission but the accusation of theft levelled against her disillusioned and shocked her extremely and led her to commit suicide. Thus the strained relation between the husband and the wife is the root of her alienation and death.

The theme of strained man-woman relation is shown not through the lives of the protagonists but through the subordinate characters in Desai's novels *Bye-Bye, Blackbird.* The relation between Adit and Sarah, the Bengali husband and the English wife is not at all strained like the relation between Sarah's parents—Mr and Mrs Roscommon James. Sarah, the mild and practical English wife of Adit, the Indian immigrant and a small agent of a tourist office in England has deep faith in and devotion to Adit. As a clever clerk she has practical knowledge and intention to adjust with her Indian husband uncaring the negligent look and bitter criticism from her neighbours who are at loggerheads with the Indian immigrants, though the husband and the wife differ in many respects. Adit has secret taste for Indian food and song in spite of his deep love for England, his golden Mecca and hate for Sarah's pet cat. Sarah also has deep love and affection for her own country under which runs her deep desire to know and come closer to India, the birth place of her husband and be Indian. That is why she chooses to accompany her husband to India after his disillusionment with England. But the relation between Sarah's parents is not happy. Sarah after her marriage is shocked to see her once-physician father reduced to the state of a beast like day labourer who is always snubbed and rebuffed by his dignified and royal wife attending to party.

The novel *Where Shall We Go This Summer?* also deals with the theme of strained man-woman relation beautifully like *Cry, the Peacock* with reference to an aged couple of reasonable husband and emotional wife. Here we have a couple living in two different psychological poles resulting in the alienation of Sita. After her father's death, Raman, a businessman of reason and rationality 'out of pity, out of lust, out of sudden will for adventure and because it was inevitable—married Sita' (99), the beloved daughter of an affluent and saintly freedom fighter who was a fraud under the skin. After Sita's marriage, she hardly feels capable of coping with her family and real social world of order and routine. In an attempt to revive the blissful dreams of childhood and free herself from the torture of mundane mainland, she decides to give her unborn baby a bewitched miraculous life, secure the magic of keeping the baby unborn and protect it from the destructive forces of modern civilization, and goes to illusory and dreamy island of her childhood. She is disheartened to see the island faded out of its childhood colour of happiness and romance. Raman comes to take her to the mainland and conquers the heart of his children who neglect their mother for her impractical wisdom. Emotional Sita is defeated by rational Raman and is led to distress. She is forced to return to the mainland of order and routine which one must accept boldly. Again the foreigner asking a lift to Ajanta in Raman's car is a trifling episode to Raman but Sita sees boldness in the foreigner and alludes to him repeatedly to Raman who is embittered by her. The young wife kissing the aged and ailing husband is a climactic happy episode to be remembered in Sita's whole life but to Raman it is too meaningless and trifling to remember. Beside the unhappy relation between the couple Raman and Sita, we have another couple to show the theme of strained man-woman relation which is darkened by secret sensuality and sexuality. Sita gradually discovered the existence of a mistress in the life of her father, a saintly freedom fighter whom the *chelas* thought to be "second Gandhi." Jiban, Sita's brother, told her that she was the step-sister of Rekha who was fondled, though sensually by her father more than Sita. He squeezed Rekha's hands and Sita always saw the oldman's hands on the shoulder of their elder sister Rekha which led Sita to gloom and wretchedness. We are also told that the father grabbed the wealth of their mother who freed herself by escaping to Benares. Thus Sita, at last realized 'what a farce marriage was, all human relationships were' (144) and confronted with the unfeeling husband 'she could hardly believe that although they lived so close together, he did not even know this basic fact of her existence' (144) that she was pained with the dullness and boredom of everyday life.

In *Fire on the Mountain* the strained relation between man-woman is not pictured directly as in the case of other novels of Anita Desai. Though the whole story of the novel is based on this particular theme of strained man-woman relation we do not see the man come in front of us in the novel physically. Nanda Kaul's husband, a Vice-Chancellor, is the indirect protagonist to pilot the agonized life of the main protagonist. The novelist has not felt any necessity to portray Nanda Kaul's husband as her first and foremost duty is to picture the psychological development and agony of the lonely life of Nanda Kaul beside her great-granddaughter Rekha who in the guise of evasion of social forces, challenges Nanda Kaul's lonely enjoyment of hilly Carignano, the Baneras of her old age and triumphs over her by dint of her intuitive quality to enjoy loneliness. Being defeated Nanda Kaul tries to rebuild a new relation with Raka. The story now takes a new turn and in the last scene the tight knot of the fantastically spun story of her father's romantic adventure to Tibet slacks. The news of the social reformer, Ila Das's death at the hands of rapist Preet Singh shocks Nanda Kaul extremely. She begins to pour out her past, and we, then, come to know that all the past memories are fantasies and cock and bull stories spun by her to satisfy Raka as well as her own bitterly-tortured lonely soul for the apathetic behaviour of her husband, the Vice-Chancellor who continued a life-long secret affair with a mathematics mistress. Thus she is forced to live a life of a woman betrayed by her husband in the field of emotion and love. Her living in Carignano is not according to her choice but a forced transportation, an elaborate attempt at self-deceit. Thus the whole drama of her life is based on her strained relation with her husband. There is also a reference to another strained man-woman relation in this novel. It is the case of Raka's drunkard father and her mother, Tara who is unhappy and beaten by her husband. So, the emotional relation between Raka's parents is not at all a happy one.

The same theme is formed in a different way in *Clear Light of Day*. Bim, the protagonist of the novel and a spinster professor of a college has to take all the responsibility of her family consisting of her unmarried and meek sister, Tara, the romantic, poetic and dauntless brother, Raja and a dumb and invalid brother, Baba beside a parasitical servant aunt Mira after the death of her parents. Tara selfishly marries a foreign diplomat, Bakul later and leaves the family and goes to Hyder Ali, the landlord and ideal hero of his childhood after his recovery from typhoid and marries Hyder Ali's youngest daughter Benazir. Bim is now left with two invalid persons to look after—one, Baba, the other Mira *masi,* the old skeletal but bonafied maidservant brought by her mother to look after baby Baba. Lonely and proud Bim is now touched to the quick for Raja's insulting letter which mercies her the rent of the same house which he himself once occupied with Bim. But she has nothing to do now but to cherish the memory of her once poetic romantic and dreamy brother, Raja who has become egoistic, materialistic, pragmatic and rational while she herself is worn out by the pressure of age, reality and responsibility. Bim's apathy and anger towards Raja subsides after Tara's coming to visit Raja's house. Tara comes to respond to his invitation at his daughter Maya's wedding. Though at first proud and stubborn Bim is shocked because heroine Bim, once closer to childhood hero, Raja is now less important to him than Tara who triumphs over her by getting Raja's invitation to his daughter's wedding. But gradually she accommodates them. Tara and Bakul try for a reconciliation between Bim and Raja and they suggest to call Raja as Bim is agonizingly overloaded with responsibility of the family and business. Bim is now revolted within. A *Clear Light of Day* haunts in the dark and suffocates the dark mind of Bim in the guise of reconciliation. She is suffused with a spiritual sense of love and affection for her brother and sister. She repents for her stubbornness and feels for her brothers and sister to forgive them and forget the past. Thus the strained relation between Bim and Raja ends in sweetness.

In *Village by the Sea* the strained man-woman relation is themed round Hari's parents. Hari's father is alcoholic and does not take care of the family which consists of three sisters—

Lila, Kamal and Bela and the brother, Hari living at Thul, a dark village under the dull and metal sun away from Bombay beside the sea. Hari, as the only conscious male member besides the drunkard father, seeks a service in Biju's boat-building factory or in the factory which is rumoured to be set up in near future. Finding no chance he joins the village march that gives slogan against the industrialization of village agriculture and arranges a deputation to Bombay. At Hari's absence Lila as the elder sister runs the family while the father drinks liquor, abuses the family members and borrows money from the neighbours only to thrust the family into deeper misery and distress. At the absence of Hari, the De Silvas, their neighbours, come to help and get their mother admitted to the hospital in exchange of the sisters' service to them. The character of Hari's father gradually develops. He leaves liquor. In course of their mother's admission to the hospital the father goes to the mother to serve and stays there till she recovers. Gradually the dark cloud of distress passes away from the family. The mother recovers from her illness. Hari earns money and returns. The flower of happiness blooms over the dark family and enlightens it. Thus though the relation between Hari's father and mother was strained earlier, it ends in sweetness. Again the father of Hari is the reprehensive of most of the Indian village fathers while the son, Hari, represents the destitute village boys.

The same theme in *In Custody* is woven with a couple of couples—impractical Deven and practical Sarla on the one hand and on the other, old decayed poet Nur, and his two wives—one, a virago with poetical imagination and dancing career and the other, ignorant with material greed for wealth. The practical wife, Sarla is a completely different character in comparison with the other emotional female characters of Anita Desai. In most of her novels it is the wives who are emotional and the husbands are reasonable but here in this novel, the husband is seen to be emotional and the creature of dreamland while the wife is practical and intellectual. Deven not only wanted to be a true disciple of Nur, the comet of Urdu poetry but also dreamt to be a glorious figure in the world of art and poetry. Sarla as a wife does not get proper information regarding Deven's glorious poetic adventure to record Nur's memoirs and has to suffer emotional as well as economic starvation. In fact it was not the realization of the dream she dreamt at youth before her marriage. Deven, for fear of opposition from his practical wife in his impractical adventure, discloses nothing as 'for the wife of a poet she seemed too prosaic' to him (67) and wastes time, money and energy wandering aimlessly from Mirpur to Delhi. He does not take proper care of his family that decays day by day. Sarla, though she does not neglect her wifely duty to her husband, is burdened with her family duty and is obliged to show apathetic look towards her husband, Deven. Thus the sweet relation is broken between them as 'it did not bring about any closeness of spirit, any comradeship' (68). Nur, the glorious Urdu poet, marries his secretary, Imtiaz Begum not only to fill up the artistic and intellectual blank of his life created by his first unintellectual wife, Safiya Begum but also to have support and service in his intellectual career and glorious poetic creation which he lacked in his first wife. But he was betrayed by the second wife who took his wealth, audience and also his poetic glory to use for her own purpose leaving the poet drained of all his possession. The poet is now seen to grieve for his mistake to Deven for the fraud of the second wife beside the first one who is foolish. Thus the relation between Nur and his wives is not at all happy one like the strained and unhappy conjugal life between Deven and Sarla. In this way the two couples contribute much to the thematic construction of the novel.

The theme of man-woman relation in *Baumgartner's Bombay* is woven in a different way than the rest of Desai's novels. In all her novels except this novel, the relation between man and woman is woven either with the help of husband-wife relation or with the help of brother-sister relation which construct the man plot of the novels. Maya-Gautama, Monisha-Jiban, Sita-Raman, Sarla-Deven and Sarah-Adit exemplify the husband-wife relation while Bim and Raja in *Clear Light of the Day* exemplify the brother-sister and Nirode and his mother exemplify the mother-son relation in *Voices in the City.* But the relation between Baumgartner and Lotte—the two Germans—one Jew in search of his livelihood anJ luck in India, driven by the ruling Nazis and the other, a cabaret dancer brought by the boatman to the bar and Grand Hotel of Calcutta, exemplifies neither of these two relations. They have neither husband-wife nor brother-sister kinship. Their sudden meeting reaches to friendship in Middleton Hotel where Lotte is exposed as impishly simple and sweetly talkative cabaret girl to young Baumgartner. But before the friendship matures the second world war is declared and from amidst a clamorous mob Lotte is whisked away by the hotel manager and Baumgartner as a German internee is taken to the internment camp after arrest and is imprisoned for six years in the heated blast furnace of prison cell. So Baumgartner and Lotte are obliged to be separated for a long time until they are reconciled in Bombay. The love-hate relation between Baumgartner and Lotte is somewhat different from other protagonists of Desai. Maya, Monisha, Sita and Nanda Kaul—all of them suffer, from emotional starvation from their husbands but Lotte and Baumgartner make sweet couple without being as couple so far we see them in the scenes of the novel. Their relation is somewhat of childish brother and sister relation resembling the first phase of Raja and Bim's life in *Clear Light of Day.* Thus without being close kinsmen the two figures 'made one comfortable whole' (82).

In *Journey to Ithaca* Desai shows the theme mainly in three ways. First, she shows it through the contrastive attitude to life of the western couple—Matteo, the Italian husband and Sophie, his German wife. In the second case she shows it through the temporary love-relation between Laila, the Egyptian girl who became the Mother and Krishna, Laila's temporary dance-master travelling Europe and America from India with his dancing troupe in search of career. In the third case the theme is woven with the help of Laila's divine love with her 'Great Sage' (300) the incarnation of God. In the first case we see that materialistic German journalist Sophie is married by Italian unsuccessful young man Matteo who journeys to India to 'study' (79) her spiritual world with Sophie. The relation between Matteo and Sophie is not at all straightforward in spite of their loyalty to each other. Having two children they differ in all respects in their attitude to life as they travel through various Indian sanctuaries. The dark, filth and superstition of the Indian ashrams indignate her. To her the worshipper Mother is a magician who draws devotees from all over the world through tricks. Matteo who is transformed to a spiritualist, a mystic, is charmed by the Mother's universal sermon coloured by divine love, universal truth, beauty and joy. To Matteo Mother's love for him is sacred while that of Sophie is profane. Mother's love is eternal, universal and formless. It is '*nirguna acintya* and Absolute' (143). Sophie's love for him is temporary and temporal. Sophie is concerned with the materialistic life and physical love while the Mother is concerned with the spiritual love. Thus the incompatible temperaments of the couple break the harmony in their conjugal life. In the second case the temporary relation between Krishna, the dance master and Laila, acting as Radha in his troupe is not bound so much with physical love as with psychological or divine love that grows through Krishna's effort for making career through dance performance and through Laila's effort for searching divine love, eternal truth, beauty and joy through Indian Radha-Krishna spiritual dance. Through spiritual dance they come physically and psychologically closer. But when Laila, the would-be mother realizes that Krishna's dance performance is more materialistic and earthly than spiritual, she tries to flee from her 'false master' (290) though they come closer to each other and enjoy a privacy behind the curtain.

In the third case Laila being disillusioned with career-maker 'false Master' (290) Krishna for his engrossment with earthly life searches for real Master, the incarnation of Almighty who would show her the way of eternal truth, beauty, divine love and joy and bring enlightenment in her dark life. In the peak of Himalayas, the 'Great Sage' (300) found by her shows her the way of enlightenment and brings eternal bliss in her life. Her relation with the real master as hinted by Dr Montuda is mystic. It is more spiritual than physical though they could not avoid physical closeness as 'Body and soul are one' (137). They enjoyed physical and spiritual union without being as social husband and wife.

The novelist through her treatment of the man-woman relation seems to suggest that extremely materialistic life is as damaging to conjugal life as extremely spiritual life which we see in the case of Sophie-Matteo relation. But the connection of both lives with human love and social service is the root of heavenly joy which we see in the case of union between Mother and her real Master.

Anita Desai's *Fasting, Feasting* is the graph of family life in two different cultures—Indian, on one hand and American, on the other. In part-I, Uma, the plain older daughter of an Indian family, is the victim of traditional system of marriage. She is cheated by Harish, the already married husband, her ignorant parents particularly Mama choose for her as Papa thought marriage as 'women's affair and left it' (82) to materially greedy Mama. Gradually Uma fails to outgrow her home and family and stays on surrounded and suffocated by godlike and masterful parents who had hardly 'been separate entities' (5). But Aruna, her dauntless and non-traditional sister, is ambitious and successful in life for a 'good' marriage. Beautiful Anamika, Aruna's cousin, is another tragic victim of marriage. She is burnt to death in her in-laws family. The picture of man-woman relation in America is somewhat different. In Part-II across the world in Massachusetts where young Arun, Uma's brother goes as a student, life outlying district of the town is bewildering and full of terror for the young Indian adolescent far from home. Here the patton family men are seen to be busy in burning pieces of flesh while their women folk do not appear to cook or eat at all. Arun is surprised with the nakedness of the Americans who starve and suffer emotionally in spite of their material wealth and freedom.

II

The most common but important illustration of the sensibility blight in Indian-writing in English is the method of portraying passion between important male and female characters. The western notion of love has darkened our consciousness about our seasoned conventions for viewing the man-woman relation and association. The classical theory does not try to formulate the emotions born out of man-woman relation with the norm of love. Philosophy offers its own vision of the urge towards sexual non-dualism which animates all cultures. In this vision both male and female principles are recognized to be integral to life and both are thought of as being subject to the same absolute which is a

Neuter. This idea of subordination of both the principles to a supreme trans sexual power is our saving idea which reminds us the western notion of love against the drift of brute sexual relation which frequently assaults and enslaves women. Though the frank guiltless erotic play of love between man and woman seems feign and contrivance in the collective touch taboo tradition of Indian-English writer tries to bind his central male and female characters into the formula of love in the western sense. In her earlier novels such as *Cry, the Peacock, Voices in the City* etc. the non-traditional and western elements of the Oriental mind act with remarkable force testing out the free ideas absorbed from the western influence and persuasions in course of the emotional play between the male and female protagonists. Both Raja Rao and Anita Desai are almost similar in their view about sex. Desai like Raja Rao, observes through the sensual love of her protagonists that sexual play is not an adequate expression of feelings. Almost all her protagonists—Maya, Monisha, Sita, Nanda Kaul tire of sex and find its emotional demand not proportionate to the real satisfaction it gives. Nirode who thinks himself to be the husband substitute of his mother hates her for her illicit relation with Major Chadha. Sita who is dissatisfied with her husband's behaviour calls her family members and neighbours 'Animals' to whom nothing but 'food' and 'sex' matter. R.K. Narayan like Raja Rao and Anita Desai is also disillusioned with sex. Raja Rao tastes love bitterly, after which abomination comes with vengeance. R.K. Narayan also tries of sex and does not find any integral use for it in the content and routine of his life. When we see Jagan in the *Vendor of Sweets* lamenting about the fever and fret of sex, we realize that his characters' disillusionment with sex is common matter and not a new discovery for them. It is a prior knowledge in their sensibility structure.

Almost all the protagonists of Desai and Raja Rao try to discover themselves through sexual passion where sexual play is a miraculous key with the help of which the novelists like Desai try to plunge into the innermost depth of human psyche. The protagonists of both the novelists are really disillusioned where the disillusionment comes with utterly dissipating significance. Desai like Raja Rao turns away from physical relation. From Nirode-Mother relation *vis-à-vis* his mother's clandestine relation with Major Chadha to Harish's incestuous marriage with destitute Uma—all the body-oriented relations fail and end in bitterness due to their extreme propensity to sensuality and sexuality. Through these complex and incestuous love-hate relations Desai seems to echo Nirode and Dharma's statement that sensual love and marriage is destructive, negative and decadent. It is 'not straightforward and pat' but coated with 'complicity' (229). It destroys people instead of liberating them. Though it is inevitable in society sexual play or physical union between man and woman arranged secretly or by marriage is not blissful or permanent if it is not tightened with the knot of mind and soul. Instead it may pollute the minds of human beings and bring danger to society. The union of soul and mind, instead of body, on the other hand, is the root of heavenly bliss to make human life meaningful as we see in the case of Baumgartner-Lotte or Mother-Master relation.

Besides, Anita Desai, like Raja Rao, tries for a sublimation of passion stripped of the element of touch. It is a kind of sublimated state of ideal love that her main protagonists especially the female ones want to enjoy beyond mere physical attachment. Maya's is the hunger for a kind of archetypal love which she wants to fulfil from Gautama. This is the hunger for a kind of love which is seen in the heavenly union of body soul and mind of 'Radha-Krishna' (25) whose name is the song lulls her, a kind of love in which the three qualities of Eternal Feminine—Mother, Hetaira and Companion—are satisfied. Monisha, Sita and Nanda Kaul—all of them have a hunger for a kind of free unquestioning self-transcending love, love in the face of human finitude, love that makes no claims and helps one to acknowledge and sublimate one's trueself. This kind of love, they think, would help them to escape from the ferocious assaults of meaningless modern existence fraught with fears and tears. This would also help them to attain authentic selfhood—the core of being which would endow a meaning to their existence. But when this kind of hunger for love is unfulfilled, they meet either physical or spiritual death, though differently. The sublimation of passion beyond the element of touch reaches its climax in Dharma-Amla relation where the thought of a physical contact or open exchange never figures in them in spite of their deep love and this is characteristically Indian behaviour deriving from segregationist traditions. Raja Rao's Madeline's apathy to touch and marriage in *Serpent and the Rope* is also an illustration of sublimated eroticism.

Both Anita Desai and Raja Rao try for sublimation of passion differently. Through their fever and fretfulness the protagonists of Rao's novels move towards a clearly perceived ideal in course of their elevated erotic play. But the protagonists of Desai's novels are lacking such clear perception in course of such emotional play. They seem to search blindly towards an indistinctly felt state of being which is beyond their acknowledgment. Amla is seen, to grope into the chaotic chasm of Dharma's love to reach to her goal. She could not realize 'what was it now that made her jump to her feet, hurry to say the farewell he had predicted, rush through the door to the wild and well-known world again?' (230).

In course of sublimation of passion both Desai and Rao reject the attempts of combining the oriental and occidental views. To Desai East is East. It is something unconquerable, untamable and intractable. It is demonic, unharnessable and frightening in comparison with the west which is small, soft and bland. In course of sublimation of passion Rao sees East in terms of calculated vengefulness. Desai sees it in terms of extreme fear and defeat which threatens her creative and sensitive soul and leads her creative faculty to a kind of denouement. In case of Desai the demonizing of East is an unuttered dirge of despondency and a sob of suppressed lament while it is dismally but successfully uttered by Raja Rao.

Apart from portraying the hazards and complexities of sexual relationships, the founding and nurturing of equality and humanity, focusing on the optimistic side of love in relation to flux and eternity of time, establishing the superiority of art and literature over science and technology, are other testing groups of Anita Desai. Man-woman relation helps her to serve these purposes.

In *Bye-Bye, Blackbird* and *Clear Light of Day*, the two pairs of couples—Sarah and Adit in the former novel and Raja and

Benazir in the latter novel—indicate Desai's change in the perspective. Through the portrayal of the former couple she tries to focus on the interracial problem arising out of the lack of racial equality for which the couple of different races suffer despite their marriage being successful unlike the unsuccessful ones of Desai's earlier novels, who suffer for themselves. The novelist seems to suggest for interracial equality and humanity through this portrayal. Besides, by making the colourless marriage of an Indian husband, Adit with an English lady, Sarah, successful in her own country that hated the black Indians, Desai seems to rescue India's lost dignity and tries to make her equal in status beside dignified England after the acquisition of her independence. Through the portrayal of the later couple Raja and Benazir, she shows a marriage between two different religious communities in a time when the nation burns with Hindu-Muslim riot. Through this portrayal, she seems to suggest secularism in India. But making the marriage of both the couples successful, the novelist seems to suggest that successful marriage, primarily, is a matter of sweet emotional bond between the husband and the wife irrespective caste, creed and religion against the arranged physical unsuccessful marriage of her earlier couples.

In *Clear Light of Day* Desai shows the optimistic side of spiritual love against the horrors and complexities of sensual love in relation to time and her characters' past memory. She seems to suggest that this kind of love can be achieved through the transcendence of one's temporal existence by which one can go beyond the flux by apprehending timeless existence within and above it. Bim perceives at last that a meaning of being can be achieved through her love for her brothers. She achieves this spiritual wholeness by choosing to bridge the rift with Raja and Baba. What the writer suggests through the sister's love to the brothers is the awareness that the powers of love not only helps in finding the answer to one's quest for meaning in life but that love and acts of love are the means of man and mankind to prevent their destruction and along with it that of history. Thus this novel portrays the novelist's optimistic attitude to love against the pessimistic one. In mot of her novels she shows love is destructive, negative and decadent. But here she shows love is creative and constructive.

In *In Custody,* the emotional conflict between the husband and the wife of her earlier novels, pales into minimum familial duty and suppressed anger leading both of them, the frustrated couple to opposite silent corners. The reason behind this paleness of personal emotional conflict is that from this novel the individual's consciousness is directed to a wider world from the world of domestic affairs. Here the novelist is concerned with the superiority of art and literature over science and technology in a materially profiteering society. Nur and Deven are bogged down by their wives' material greed and mercenary exploitation of art and literature in a science and technology-dominated society.

The two novels—*The Village by the Sea* and *Baumgartner's Bombay*—also show the novelist's change in the perspective in relation to this theme. In *The Village by the Sea* the novelist portrays the suffering of humanity due to the problem of inequality in socio-economic condition. So she brings Hari's parents' poverty-stricken condition though the father's drunkenness beyond poverty may be considered a little responsible for their suffering. In *Baumgartner's Bombay* also the novelist portrays the human suffering. But the reason of this suffering is different from the former novel. Here the suffering is due to the flaw of fanaticism. The suffering of Baumgartner, the representative male victim, and that of Lotte, the representative female victim, are due to the fanaticism of the Nazis and the Jews. Desai seems to vindicate socialism through *The Village by the Sea* and secularism through *Baumgartner's Bombay.* In both the novels the novelist serves her purposes in terms of man-woman relation which is a fine technique for her to shape the story and pattern of all the novels.

WORKS CITED

Desai, Anita. *Baumgartner's Bombay.* London: William Heinemann, 1988.

——. *Cry, the Peacock.* Delhi: Orient Paperbacks, 1980.

——. *Fasting, Feasting.* London: Chatto & Windus, 1999.

——. *In Custody.* New York: Harper and Row, 1984.

——. *Journey to Ithaca.* London: William Heinemann, 1995.

——. *Voices in the City.* Delhi. Orient Paperbacks, 1965.

——. *Where Shall We Go This Summer?* New Delhi: Orient Paperbacks, 1982.

10

WHEN DREAMS TRAVEL: 'WRITING BACK' TO *THE ARABIAN NIGHTS*

MOHUA GHOSH

I

The Arabian Nights is a well-known canonized text which most of us are familiar with. Githa Hariharan's *When Dreams Travel* calls back to and illuminates this old story with a new look. We appreciate this new novel and enjoy reading it as a recognition of the hidden text comes at frequent turns of the novel.

We are frequently placed in a quasi-historic or legendary past as we travel through Hariharan's 'Dreams.' In overlapping the locational sites of the past with that of the present, the author does not always follow the demands of conventional realism. So, the past-present-future mingle in her consciousness creating and inventing her own traveling dreams.

The Thousand and One Nights is a collection of stories incorporating romances, fairy tales and legends, parables and fables, and both exotic and realistic adventures. Now there is a story behind the existence and creation of these stories. This book evolved through a period of more than eight centuries. The frame story is about Sultan Shahryar of Shahabad and his younger brother Shahzaman, ruler of Samarkhand. Both were happy and contended with their subjects and their life went on smoothly. Once after many years the younger brother is invited to visit Shahabad. Rejoiced at the prospect of meeting his elder brother, Shahzaman makes elaborate preparations for the journey. Just out of his city-palace, he camps for the night to begin the journey at early dawn. At night he remembers about a special gift, which was left at the palace. Silently Shahzaman steals out into the dark night and enters his palace. Entering his bedroom, he is shocked at the sight of his beautiful queen sleeping peacefully in the embrace of a black slave. The scene at first blurs his vision and senses. But the dangling sword in front of him hastens his action. Within a moment, the royal bed overflows with blood and wiping the sword back to its place, the ruler comes back to his camp. Without waiting for dawn, he orders his men to set out immediately for Shahabad.

Reaching his brother's city gates, he receives a warm welcome and a grand honour. But Sultan Shahryar is worried at his younger brother's pale sorrowful features. On asking him, he does not get a definite answer and thinks that it was due to the long strenuous journey. The Sultan however arranges for a hunting expedition to entertain his brother but Shahzaman refuse to participate. Roaming alone in the palace, he witnesses a horrible sight. He sees his sister-in-law, the queen of Shahabad engaged in naked lecherous activities inside the palace-garden along with other slave girls and black slaves. This sight stuns him at first but then he comforts himself with the thought that he is not the only husband betrayed and cuckolded. His elder brother's misfortune is greater than his. These thoughts revive him and relieve him of his grim mental state. The Sultan, returning from his trip, is surprised at the sudden change of his brother and becomes anxious to learn the cause. After much persuasion, Shahzaman is forced to narrate in details everything starting from his own life-experiences to what he has visualized recently in his brother's palace. Shahryar refuses to believe the unfaithfulness of his noble queen. So, the younger brother suggests to secretly spy on the queen. The Sultan is full of agony to view such a sight in his own palace. But instead of bloodshed, he proposes to renounce the world till he meets another person suffering from such disgrace. Shahzaman agrees with his elder and the brothers travel far and wide.

They reach a sea-shore and rest under a tree. Suddenly they see something huge and black rising out of the sea. Terror-stricken, they climb up a tree and see a giant come out of the sea with a large chest on his head. Wonder-struck, the brothers watch a beautiful young lady come out of the box. The giant with a satisfactory look at her goes to sleep on the woman's lap. The girl tells her story of being carried away by this giant on her bridal night when she was still a virgin. Since then, she has been befooling the giant in his presence, thus being able to take revenge despite being imprisoned.

This incident leaves such an impact on the two brothers that they decide to return to their royal life. Loathing all womankind, Shahryar first orders the execution of his wife, the woman-slaves and their black lovers. Then he hits on a hideous plan of marrying a virgin every night and after deflowering her, kills her the next morning. This new policy creates a panic in the kingdom. A time comes when no more candidates are left to marry and to be killed. However the Wazir's daughter Shaharzada, devises a scheme to save herself and others and insists her father to arrange her marriage with the king. Each night she tells a story, leaving it incomplete and promising to finish it the following night. The stories are so entertaining, and the king is so eager to hear the end that he puts off her execution from day to day and finally abandons his cruel plan. This story-telling continues for a thousand and one nights after which the Sultan is cured of his obsession against women. Dunyazad, the younger sister, is married to Shahzaman and 'The Thousand and One Nights' end with an emphatic promise that the couples will live happily hereafter.

Githa Hariharan retains this above frame as she begins her novel *When Dreams Travel.* But she deals with the untold details of the legend and questions the many complacent assumptions of the original text.

The novel consists of two parts. Part One is called 'Travellers' and Part Two—'Virgins, Martyrs and Others.' In the first chapter of Part One titled 'In the Embrace of Darkness,' the author re-tells the age-old beginning of the Arabian Nights. But that her story is different from the legend is clearly indicated in the last line of the first chapter: "The story ends on-stage. Off-stage it has just begun" (16).

Hariharan's story begins in the second chapter "On the Way to Paradise." The two titles appear to carry a subtle suggestion that the characters of the age-old legend emerging from the 'darkness' of orthodox patriarchal tyranny travel towards a healthy environment of 'Paradise' through our author's imagination. It may also be ironical, since the so-called 'Paradise' proves to be only illusory.

The thousand and one nights' storytelling is over. With it the people are relieved of the panic of bloodshed. Peace and prosperity rules the empire. The author gives the picture of the royal gardens where the two couples sit facing each other. The two brothers, the once ruthless rulers have turned into living responsible husbands. But the author is ironical about the description of their queens—the two sisters, Shahrzad and Dunyazad, who once saved themselves and the entire kingdom risking their lives, with their creative power. They are quiet and silent now when there's no sword dangling over their heads. The Sultan now returning to his senses, wants to know the source of Shahrzad's wonderful variety of stories. He is now loyal and tender toward his queen and he is eager to know about her dreams and her free spirit. But Shahrzad is seen here bold and self-confident, and also satirical in answering her Sultan. She is no more the new bride of the old legend compelled to talk out for her life. She replies modestly but briefly that her dreams are nothing extraordinary to be narrated and they can only be realized and felt by those imprisoned in hovels or having their lives at risk. Shahrzad is the saviour queen now, admired and praised by the common people as well as by the Sultan. She seems silent now as her task of storytelling as well as redemption is over. We also come to know about the children of the Sultan Shahryar and his begum Shahrzad who are grown-ups now. A celebration of the marriage of Dunyazad and Shahzaman adds to the happiness that reigns over the kingdom after the nights of terror.

When Dreams Travel questions this apparent happiness and shifts to another fifteen and twenty years after the marriage celebration. Hariharan deliberately remains uncertain about the time but continuously looks back to the thousand nights while narrating subsequent events. Dunyazad, now a widow, receives the news of her sister's death and decides to visit the old palace of Shahabad, festered with memories. She has learnt many things from her famous sister and seems to walk in her footsteps as she partakes on the journey from her palace at Samarkhand to Shahabad. Dunyazad in male disguise reaches the old palace.

Then begins the 'Knots in the afterlife' of Sultan Shahryar and the now widowed Dunyazad. She reaches the palace and meets Sahiba, the old nurse-maid. She seems changed now after so many years. She undresses Dunyazad from her male disguise and she looks like an ageing princess. Self-consciously she ruminates the past and finds that the room she is brought into is not one of the old ones. She tries to rouse the past in Sahiba who sighs about the lack of children in the royal palace. Dunyazad does not even remember the dead children of her sister nor the lone survivor Prince Umar. However, interrupting the nurse-maid's nostalgic fit, she asks her long suppressed question about the death of her sister. But Sahiba refuses to give a satisfactory answer even after persuasion. Dunyazad anticipates a mystery lurking behind the death of her sister. She paces up and down the room thinking of the past memories and the present situation.

A message from Sultan Shahryar comes to Dunyazad. For a moment she is in a dilemma about meeting her brother-in-law, but agrees at last. The whole night she dreams of traveling through tunnels and palaces as if in search of something. In her dream she finds the tomb of her sister but feels a menacing grief at not finding even a mention of her own name on the famous tomb. The next morning Dunyazad swims down memory-lane to her father, to the hour of the Wazir's death and the day when her sister came to be the saviour queen along with her as her constant companion. We are brought back to the present suddenly as Dunyazad, with the help of the slave-girl Dilshad, gets ready to meet the Sultan. She feels foolish to be anxious to meet her very-known brother-in-law. Yet Dunyazad feels demeaned.

The two intimately known persons meet at the same place where they had met in the past but this is the first time they do so in the absence of Shahrzad. Dunyazad's mind flashes with the varied images of the Sultan she had witnessed and now compares those with the present faded melancholy appearance of the royal person. Shahryar seems a stranger to her with wrinkled skin and sunken cheeks. The Sultan starts speaking about his precious love for his queen and how he would show it to the world. They roam about the palace rooms together, the Sultan speaking and Dunyazad being the silent listener again. During their next meeting, Dunyazad gathers up courage to ask about Prince Umar. But the question brings out the old despot in Shahryar. He sharply comments about the imbecile son of Dunyazad and her stepson being on the throne and again continues to speak of his love for Shahrzad. Dunyazad feels enraged at such boastings and blurts out her doubts about her sister's death. The situation becomes intriguing when Shahryar, instead of answering Dunyazad's queries, wants to know about his brother Shahzaman's death. Both the widow and the widower silently challenge each other adding further knots to their lives.

On the other hand Dilshad and Dunyazad come closer to each other. Dilshad confides in Dunyazad about the ornate wooden chest of Shahrzad, which the Sultan himself gave her. The old ivory-framed mirror comes out. Dunyazad alone in her room sees into the mirror just like her sister. It seems she sees a reflection of her self, which is very different from that of the image of the saviour queen.

The hammam recalls the old sweet memories of Dunyazad when both the sisters would come there with their mother, safe and protected within her arms. The sweet memories drift into sad ones like her mother Raziya's death. Hariharan here presents the silent and supposedly agreeable Raziya as a silent rebel who had also yearned to claim and demand for herself, for her own daughters. Once separated, the mother and the daughters had never met. Dunyazad now recalls and imagines her mother wanting to protest, to scream in anger against the injustice done to her daughters. Thus the daughter sees not the broken heart of a mother but the outrage and explosion of a long subdued human being. Dunyazad meets Prince Umar with the help of the wily slave girl Dilshad. To Dunyazad, her nephew seems to reflect the spirit of her father, the Wazir and her mother Raziya. She cannot find anything of the Sultan in the young boy. The young prince is goaded by an ardent passion for his kingdom and its well-being. He also talks about his love for his mother but as if she is dead and gone. This is what troubles Dunyazad. She cannot think how can someone who is loved by another completely disappear from the latter's life.

Dunyazad, so long curious about the peculiar date-shaped mark at the side of Dilshad's mouth, asks about it one day when she was caressed by the slave-girl. She narrates how it was a gift from a freakish poet Satyasama. She was a rare slave brought to the King's court. She had sleek fur all over her body and was a wandering poet in her own country. Her too truthful verses offended the king and she was ordered death. But the executioner, out of sympathy did not kill the poet-girl. Her neck was ringed and voice changed forever but she was put into a merchant's boat to be far away from her country. She became a favourite of Shahryar's court with her strange poetic entertainments and also fell in love with one of the eunuchs guarding the harem. This was a grim offence and she was imprisoned in a windowless room. Her passion was the sky, the clear sky with no bounds. And without being able to see the sky, the poet began to fade away. Dilshad was her nurse then in whose arms the poet died giving her a parting kiss. Dilshad seems to carry this mark on her face as if keeping alive the poet who spoke out strange truths.

With the help of Dilshad, Prince Umar is able to usurp the throne of his father. The Prince along with his rebel followers captures Shahryar in the mausoleum built for Shahrzad. Dilshad and Dunyazad were also there along with the Sultan. The Sultan is imprisoned in the mausoleum of his own creation. Dunyazad feels that she need not stay any more in the palace at Shahabad and prepares for her return journey to Samarkhand. The first part of the novel ends here.

The second part of the novel 'Virgins, Martyrs and Others' shows a shift from 'memory-making' to 'storytelling.' The first chapter 'A Dream, A Mirror' again starts with the four figures in the night's embrace. But this time we see a change of the storytellers and the listeners too. The ruthless rulers are absent and the storytellers are accompanied by two goading jinns, one Shahrzad and the other Satyasama. Discarding the oppressive, self-centred, insensitive males who can neither acknowledge nor attribute any recognition to a creative genius, Githa Hariharan seems to bring together the innovative, creative spirits that lie concealed and suppressed in women. The story-tellers, Dunyazad and the slave-girl Dilshad, are midway between Shahabad and Samarkhand. They decide to re-enact the entire event of storytelling for seven days and nights during their sojourn in the desert. But now they are free without any fear of their heads being chopped off and can tell each other their own pasts, dreams, their future plans and reinvent their lives.

Dunyazad's first story is 'Rowing a Floating Island' where she tells about the personal sufferings of Shahrzad which were untold in *The Arabian Nights.* Shahrzad's compulsive biological procreation is vividly portrayed here. Her few moments of joy and excitement of being a mother, again her anxiety to reach the Sultan's bed-chamber at the scheduled hour even on the delivery day and her prolonged frustration and sufferings are voiced through Dunyazad's story.

Dilshad tells stories not about male fantasies and adventures but about some women, their talents and innovations, their joy and creation and their punishments and sufferings for their talents. She narrates how Satyasama, the poet who wanted to see the sky was turned into a monkey-face, later one-eyed and finally remaining only a moaning voice of the city.

Stories go on 'A Lover, a Tomb' of Dunyazad shows Shahryar's sufferings after being deposed by his son. The once tyrant ruler instead of being repentant, suffers from a sense of unease, now being imprisoned in the 'immortal' tomb of his own making. But his days are also numbered. However he is not at all remorseful for the three years of bloodshed and murder that he had unleashed in the past. The Sultan reigned complacently both before and after these bloody years without any difference. Furthermore, he is self-conceited at the reprieve he sanctioned to Shahrzad after the thousand and one nights. As if, it was he, who made Shahrzad the martyr, and heroine of his kingdom and eventually he too came to admire this woman but for her chastity only. And one day when he realized that the chaste Sultana was turning wily, he felt that the two of them couldn't win at the same time. One must lose the game. Just after this Shahrzad disappeared from his life and he 'mourned' her deeply by building the grand mausoleum in her memory.

In this way Dunyazad's stories come out as reminiscences of the thousand and one nights and Dilshad carried on with her accounts of the strange tales of Rupavati's breasts, how she became a man Rupavata who was actually the Buddha-to-be. We also get from her stories of flight and fancy about the Nanni, a poor goat-herd, the strange women Poison-skin, Lonely Voice etc. The last chapter of this novel, the story by Dilshad 'The Morning After' comes as a big surprise to the readers. We witness Shahrzad, the saviour queen still alive. Much of this novel is concerned, with Dunyazad's efforts to find out the causes and happenings of the mysterious death of Shahrzad. The truth is revealed in the last chapter.

Shahrzad is now a feeble old woman left to the care of the slave-girls in a remote corner of the palace. She resurrects her past, her turning into a martyr from a virgin, how her quick wit and felicitous tongue beguiled the Sultan and saved herself and the entire Shahabad from destruction. But now she is worried about the present generation of women. What will they do if the sword now blunt and rusted suddenly wishes to dazzle and be sharpened? Hariharan does not conclude but ends her novel with this apprehension about the future of women.

Thus we see that Githa Hariharan's *When Dreams Travel* exists in referentiality to the original text of the *The Arabian* Nights, along with significant echoes and more significant departures. She crystallizes the elements of the legend to write her own novel, which is a ceaseless pursuit of truth about the making of a fiction or a story, which is essentially 'Her Story.'

II

Throughout the original text women are presented as lustful objects whose only aim is to debauch and befool men, specially their husbands. But no one felt it necessary to search the cause for such behaviour on the part of women. It was taken for granted that Sultans could fill their harems, and even ordinary men could have many wives. Thus women had no identity, no creative space for herself. They received neither love nor any dignity as wives from their husbands. Perhaps to satisfy their natural physical urge and at the same time a latent sense of revenge against the male chauvinism, they behaved in such an illegitimate manner.

Githa Hariharan in *When Dreams Travel* brings out this answer by exposing the sadism and cynicism behind the androcentric myth about harems: "All kings are collectors. These valuable items are women of all shapes, colours, sizes" (90). And after callously dumping their properties behind the stone walls of the palace the kings would propagate the myth—"The harem breeds hungry women, a race of cuckolding subjects" (78). Even Shahrzad's act of storytelling is projected by the author as her desperate struggle to survive entrapment by a cruel patriarchal orthodoxy. It is the anguish of the imprisoned genius that comes to focus while reading *When Dreams Travel* instead of the charming adventure tales of males *of Arabian Nights*:

> Only those locked up in hovels and dungeons and palaces can see and hear these dreams. Only those whose necks are naked and at risk can understand them. (20)

Thus we envision an act of '*ecriture feminine*' in the creativity of Shahrzad that is her power and happiness. So, Githa Hariharan observes:

> The powerless have a dream or two, dreams that break walls, dreams that go through walls as if they are powerless. (25)

This suggestion of woman's power is also covertly mentioned in the original text, which the author of *When Dreams Travel* deconstructively brings out:

> He (the Sultan) has been brought to senses by *a woman* [...] with *her* stories. (21)

At the same time she is ironical in representing the attitude of Shahryar, at the supposed death of his saviour queen. The king mourns her death in his magnificent mausoleum not for her powerful creativity and talent but only for being pure and chaste. So, the queen's ecriture is dismissed without being acknowledged, and she is gauged in the male world on the basis of the patriarchal value of chastity, imposed exclusively on women.

We can perceive the futility and banality of the real life of these women behind the original stories, through the author's penetrating feministic insight. She rewrites the legend in the post-modern context of feminism by vividly emphasizing the pain of the woman and the cruelty that was perpetrated on her. The queen's act of telling interesting stories is seen here as an act of compulsion imposed upon her by the abject male chauvinism robbing her dignity and life. A frenzied storyteller of *When Dreams Travel*, Shahrzad has no room of her own, not even the attic reserved for the 'madwoman.' She is a prisoner of her harem during the day. At night the lecherous powerful patriarch's dungeon is her grim nuptial bed, epitomizing the terror and grime of her marital life. Shahrzad has no respite from this ugly unwashed bed smeared with blood, sweat and semen even when she gives birth to a child during the day. As a wife, she stands nowhere, just another addition to the line of previous brides who had been raped in the dark and killed at dawn. Even as a mother, the queen fails to attain her selfhood. She is not allowed to experience the bliss and joy of fulfilment of motherhood as the newborn babe is handed over to the nurses to be reared in another corner of the palace. With the sword hanging over the head, Shahrzad is forced to continue her creation and procreation.

Again, the original tale silences this queen as just another member of the harem after the end of thousand and one nights. The king's salvation with their so-called happiness is resented by the author in *When Dreams Travel.* Githa Hariharan does not forget this invisible and inaudible Shahrzad. She questions persistently:

> What will happen to you Shahrzad, when the urgent need for storytelling [...] is withdrawn? Will you be satisfied with bed time tales to your children. (133)

That the undaunted consummate artist should return to petty domesticity, is natural to the patriarchal complacency. But the absurdity of this forcible silencing troubles the modern conscious feminist author:

> The mistake, of course, is to imagine that a happy ending is possible when you have survived a shipwreck in a sea of blood. Shahryar should have killed himself in remorse, or at least renounced the city and the world, become a mad hermit in the desert. And Shahrzad? Can life continue, static, peopled with little events, commonplace milestones, after martyrdom? (105)

So, she takes it upon herself to challenge and reject the androcentric imagination by inventing a story about the later events and experiences in the life of the storyteller. And Hariharan warns:

> The story ends en-stage. Off-stage it has just begun. (16)

When Dreams Travel begins long after *The Thousand and One Nights* ends when Dunyazad, the younger sister receiving the death news of her elder sister undertakes a long journey in male disguise from Samarkhand to Shahabad. But a stunning disclosure awaits towards the end of the novel. We stumble across an old forgotten woman left to the care of the slave-girls in a remote corner of the palace. This enfeebled woman appearing in the grey morning is none but the queen Shahrzad supposed or broadcasted to be dead long ago by her polygamous husband. To this selfish monarch, Shahrzad as an individual might have been as good as dead.

But Hariharan makes Shahrzad emerge as the epitome of conscious feminist effort for survival in a society, which is hostile to, and annihilating for women. So, in the last chapter "The Morning After" we get a vision of another Shahrzad, who has passed the prime of her youth and life. She looks back and forth with a feeling of joy and anxiety mixed for the unself-conscious slave girls. She is happy that her stories saved the grandmas of these girls from the cruel lust of the Sultan. Again she is anxious about their future as her past and present experiences merge into one another, "a circle with no beginning or end" (256). She has won a personal battle no doubt with her pioneering female voice and saved many women from death. But what about their ignominy? There is no end to the custom of filling up of harems. The few rights, which the queen acquired through her partial victory are but precarious. Any time the situation may get reversed. She is apprehensive about the real dangers lurking behind "The Morning After." So, this disturbed old queen warns her present generation to remain alert to her forebodings so that they can accept the challenge when their turn comes:

> [...] When the drums roll, and the sword blunted with age, the rusty, wake up to be freshly sharpened? (276)

In *When Dreams Travel* Hariharan also brings to focus other past events and people, specially the silenced women whom the original text merely cut off from their pages. The Wazir's wife who is the mother of the two brave daughters Shahrzad and Dunyazad, the mother of Shahryar, the slave girls and maids of the palace and the younger sister Dunyazad are allowed to surface here with their individual pleasures and pains. Their pain of being wrenched apart and orphaned is felt intensely by the author. In her characteristic satiric-ironic style she points out the indifference of the Arabian legends towards the mothers of the kings. Shahryar and Shahzaman—the epitomes of unlimited patriarchal powers, of the orthodox society—also needed the services of a mother:

> before they mounted their steeds, snapped their fingers to summon waiting slaves. (8)

But the original male text has no space to honour the mother's contribution or their wishes. We get a glimpse of Raziya in *When Dreams Travel,* the mother of Shahrzad and Dunyazad who is forced to silence. But Githa Hariharan deliberately points out her bitter despair, her hopelessness and outrage through Dunyazad's vision of her mother years later. The death of this subdued and imperceptible mother was explained as the natural consequence of a broken heart. But through Dunyazad's eyes, Hariharan shows a different image:

> She saw her mother's heart for a moment before it was shrouded from sight and buried forever. And what she saw was not a broken spring, but a chamber where outrage swelled the air, stretched it to grotesque dimensions till the tightly packed, thin skinned balloon of a place exploded the aftermath of an enraged heart. (84)

Dunyazad, always behind the curtain in *The Arabian Nights,* is also made to assert her identity as a woman in *When Dreams Travel.* Githa Hariharan ironically points out her role as one who is always expected to wait upon her elder sister and the monarch. She is destined for the requirements of others. Even she forgot to dress according to her heart's content. She had to be dressed according to rules—first as a 'handmaiden' to Shahrzad and Shahryar, then like Shahzaman's wife, a queen. Later like a widow and guardian to the boy-king of her kingdom. Even being a kingmaker, "her power will always be circumscribed by her invisibility" (198) and she will be relegated to the "respectable background" (199) as quickly as possible.

Hariharan makes Dunyazad look back years later to the thousand and one nights and resurrects the past only to subvert it through ironical retelling of tales and re-discovering of shocking surprises. We feel her discontent when she realizes that her elder sister Shahrzad was always on the forefront although her contribution in the art of tale-telling is not to be ignored. The '*feminine ecriture*' which goes unrecognized in the case of Shahrzad achieves a stand in the 'dreams' and 'mirrors' of Dunyazad and Dilshad, a slave girl. Dunyazad looking back at Shahrzad's creativity may also be considered in the light of Alice Walker's 'daughter' (figure) who is in search of the 'garden' of her 'mother' (figures). For seven days and nights they tell each other stories, their own stories, not those of the golden legend. They try to re-enact and revive Shahrzad who had saved them through her fictions. These two women silenced in the source text take turns to play the roles of their saviour queens in *When Dreams Travel.* Through these two female storytellers, the author rewrites "the macrocosmic metanarrative of the thousand and one nights in the microcosmic form, from a post-modern context of feminism and metafiction" (Kundu). These two new frame-narrators reconstruct their individual past through their sad, absurd often horrifying magic stories of strange women. They also bring to light their hidden terror and sadness and their moments of daring and subsequent banality. However they succeed in asserting their identity as women through their magic-realistic tales.

The author of *When Dreams Travel* is uncertain about the place of women in today's world. The pervasive rise of fundamentalism pins woman as its worst victim suggesting that her situation is a continuing reality through time and space. She wonders about further grim eventualities, which may be in store for this 'second sex.' Thus Hariharan does not conclude but ends her story connecting feminism with post-feminism evoking the struggle of the earlier women to caution the future ones to remain conscious.

WORKS CITED

Tales From 1001 Arabian Nights. (Selected from the original sixteen volumes of the book of *The Thousand Nights And a Night*). Trans. Sir Richard F. Burton. 7th ed. Mumbai, Delhi: Jaico Publishing House, 1999.

Currie, M. (ed.). *Metafiction.* London: Longman Group Ltd., 1995.

Hariharan, Githa. *When Dreams Travel.* London: Picador, 1999.

Hutcheon, L. "Histographic Metafiction" in Currie, M. (ed.). *Metafiction.* London: Longman Group Ltd., 1995.

Kundu, R. "Githa Hariharan: Intertext, Metafiction and 'Her Story' in *Post Independence Indian English Fiction* (Eds. R. Mittapalli and Alessandro Monti). New Delhi: Atlantic Publishers and Distributors, 2001.

11

FEMINIST INTERROGATION OF A PATRIARCHAL TEXT: INTERTEXTUAL ECHOES AND DEPARTURES

MOHUA GHOSH

Githa Hariharan's *When Dreams Travel* (1999) reverberates with echoes from *The Arabian Nights.* The four main characters—emperor Shahryar, his brother Shahzaman, and the two sisters, Shaharzada and Dunyazad—of the legendary tale are also the protagonists of Githa Hariharan's *When Dreams Travel.* There are also other common characters like the Wazir, Sahiba, the nurse-maid, the slave-girls, and common places of action like the king's palace at Shahabad and that of his brother at Samarkhand.

The background of the novel is the old popular tale. The chapter entitled 'In the Embrace of Darkness' in Part I—'Travellers' of the novel relates the age-old story of how the thousand and one tales were told by the bride Shaharzada to the Emperor Shahryar. The actual story begins, Githa Hariharan makes it clear, after thousand and one nights have passed when the emperor unites with his bride, acknowledging that his decision of killing women after marrying for a night was wrong. Next the author travels in and out of the lives of these four characters, from the chapter 'On the Way to Paradise.' She spans medieval to contemporary times through a spellbinding range of stories, which are dark, poetic and witty in turn. Thus in this novel we have a sharp and lively blend of the past and present and a skilful reworking of the historical tradition.

The world famous *The Thousand and One Nights* is a typical story within a story. *The Encyclopedia Britannica* classifies it as Islamic folk literature in which variegated materials like adventure, romances, fables, anecdotes, etc. are set within a frame story. The scene of this frame story is Central Asia or "the islands or peninsulae of India and China." Within this frame we see tales continuously being told within tales. Shaharzada, the newly-wed bride of the Sultan Shahryar starts telling stories under the shadow of death. But different stories come within her story by various narrators. In *The Arabian Nights* we come across a series of stories whose first narrator was the Wazir trying to persuade his daughter about the dangers of marrying the Sultan. Within his story, a fisherman tells a story to a Ifrit about king Yunan who again tells a story to his minister, who in turn narrates a story to a sage. Again we see the Sultan narrating the adventures of Sinbad and his falcon, to his Wazir who again tells the tale of the Husband and the Parrot. Within that story we find another minister telling story to the King about the Prince and the Ogress. Hariharan also retains the above frame in her novel but with certain departures.

Within the frame of double fiction, our author finds it easier to tell a story about storytelling—a woman telling the story about the search for her own identity. This familiar device of stories within stories is common throughout literary history through which Hariharan can internalize the relationship between authors and readers, art and life. This helps her to raise metafictional issues as her novel includes within itself a fiction as well as a criticism of that fiction.

Githa Hariharan beautifully portrays the picture of the orthodox society of the famous legend using it as the backdrop of her novel. *When Dreams Travel* brings to life the violent atrocities and injustice inflicted upon women to suggest that the situation of the female class has not yet improved. Throughout time and space it has been a continuing reality.

Like *The Thousand and One Nights,* we find the characters of *When Dreams Travel* accompanied by the host of jinns and ghosts at every point of their lives. The novel is full of magic and varied narrative styles like that of the old fairy tale. While reading this novel, we can recollect the real and imaginary travels, past and present, glorious etymologies of names of the Arabian Nights. Along with the author we travel across the islands or peninsulae of India, China and Central Asia. The characters belong to the realm of myth and legend.

The stories we come across in *The Arabian Nights* were all orally transmitted by different characters. So, they were all the reconstruction from their memories, a product of their own innovative spirits. This profusion of creation is also echoed in *When Dreams Travel* where the storytellers, both the former and the later, prove themselves to be artists weaving on tales after tales.

The common storyteller at the beginning of both the novel and the legend is the bride Shaharzada. But as we progress further we see departures in *When Dreams Travel* where the once mute listeners become tellers. In the *Arabian Nights* the main speaker is Shaharzada while in the course of stories within stories, various other storytellers come to focus. In *When Dreams Travel* however, the number of storytellers has been kept down to three: at first Shaharzada and then Dunyazad and Dilshad. This is because here the author's emphasis is not on the stories in particular but rather on the speakers and their lives—their dreams and wishes, longings and frustrations.

The listeners of the exotic tales are the two brothers,—Shahryar and Shahzaman,—and Dunyazad, the accomplice of the new bride. Later we see their roles change in *When Dreams Travel.* Always they are in the embrace of darkness. The stories and most of the actions of the novel take place at night when 'the moon's sickle shaped mouth is stretched tight in a thin smile.'

The stories told in the legend and the novels are completely different. In the *Arabian Nights* the stories told are all related to male adventures and heroism. But they represented women as wicked, traitors and debauchees, cruel and witch-like although they were supposedly told by a woman. Though this aspect is absent in *When Dreams Travel* in both the tales we see the stories pointing to the fact that women are objects of desire only. They are denied any sort of identity and recognition despite their talents. Even having such talents as to surpass men was considered an offence and women were tortured and cruelly punished for that. In the original text this is taken for granted; in the modern text this has been probed and challenged.

The events and characters of *The Arabian Nights* take us to the mystic land charming one into acquiescence. Starting reading *When Dreams Travel* we are also enraptured by the fantasy and wonder, the richness of imagery and the seductiveness of the prose. But as we go through the novel inevitable questions surface from the apparently harmless fairy tales. Hariharan begins with the same dreamy palace and the same royal characters with their previous life-experiences but we stumble to a sudden halt when she says, "The story ends on-stage. Off-stage it has just begun" (16). Thus the author while echoing the legend, voices her own critique of the same through the deliberate departures.

The organization of the novel *When Dreams Travel* demonstrates Githa Hariharan's control of the fictional craft. The book's carefully planned structure with its daring lines of departure from the source text brings out its submerged sub-text of pain and cruelty. The author in her novel challenges and at the same time rejects the discourses of the earlier text to undercut male textuality. While catching the echoes of the harmless tales of *The Arabian Nights,* Hariharan breaks it open, deviates from it and disintegrating the male assumptions, subverts the previous work, creating something fresh and novel.

This post-modern use of the device of 'Intertext' helps the author to voice her feminist protests through rewriting the sexist assumptions of the past, in a new context. In her attempt to do so, she takes recourse to several devices like parody, metafiction etc.

When Dreams Travel begins with the same frame story as that of *The Thousand and One Nights* but with a difference. The story telling bride Shaharzada weaving on tales for a thousand and one nights under the shadow of death is repeatedly alluded to in course of this novel. But whereas the stories were of greater interest in *The Arabian Nights,* here it is the storyteller who draws our attention. As Dunyazad, the younger sister is made to look back years later to the thousand and one nights, "She sees that it was always Shaharzada who was its central magnetic figure" (105). Githa Hariharan does not deal with the fantastic tales of male adventures, ambitions and triumphs of the legend. Rather she brings out the soul of the human individual, not just a female storyteller. The legend used her merely as a handy prop on which a large number of readymade stories could be hung. But Hariharan presents her as a full-fledged flesh and blood human individual having her own desires and dreams, her pains and frustrations. The author directly attacks the well-known scene of storytelling of *The Arabian Nights* as 'shamelessly immortal' (7). The things which remained suppressed under the fantasy of *The Arabian Nights* are boldly brought forth in this novel. The readers of the famous novel are brought down from their colourful flights of fancy to this hard earth of reality when they are made to feel the amount of torture and injustice dealt out to the young bride. Was it really her idea to tell stories and even then, how could she keep herself alive for a thousand and one nights when none other had managed to elude death? We also wonder how this presumably well-brought up girl, could have such a store of down-to-earth knowledge and from where did she know so many stories? Hariharan very cleverly rouses such questions in the minds of the readers. Within this frame she also criticizes the earlier text for remaining vague about the parents of the Sultans and the geographical locations of the place. And she specially points out the total absence of the mother in the legend. Her tone of satire is evident when she says that Shahryar and Shahzaman, though now kings and Sultans, required a mother when they were infants. "As for the mother (or mothers of Sultans) the storyteller is completely silent on the point. Surely Shahryar and Shahzaman must have required the services of a mother before they mounted their steeds" (8). But the legend, obviously written by a male in an orthodox patriarchal background considers a mother nothing but a child-bearing medium. So, the storywriter remained deliberately silent about such a character who haunts our feminist author and also the modern readers.

The Thousand and One Nights concludes with a grand celebration all over the kingdom as the king is cured of his obsession against women. Marriages occur with an emphatic promise that the couples will live happily ever after. But Hariharan questions the validity of this assumption "The mistake of course, is to imagine that a happy ending is possible when you have survived a shipwreck in a sea of blood" (105). So, rejecting the time frame of the legend, she starts her novel long after those dreadful nights are over. And she deliberately remains vague about the time. "Yet in some years, say fifteen, twenty, the news travels to Samarkand [...]" (22). Her story starts with the journey of Dunyazad in male disguise. She is a widow now and learning about her sister Shaharzada's sudden death, she decides to take up the journey, which the author mentions is about fifteen and twenty years. The author imagines the future events long after the famed nights and describes them in her novel. She wonders how could a ruler—and what sort of a man he might be—marry a virgin every night, rob her virginity and kill her the next morning. And after performing this grisly task continuously for three years, how could this same man, though he may be a Sultan, lead a normal conjugal life of love and faith. Hariharan considers the ending of the legend absurd because such a man after salvation from a dreadful involvement is bound to become either mad or a hermit renouncing the world or at the worst can commit suicide. But the legend does not express the least remorse on the part of this ruthless man. Rather, the patriarchal society celebrates the self-conceited Sultan who thinks he has done a great job in doing away with his horrible whims and at last saving Shaharzada and the succeeding generation of women from untimely deaths. Hariharan expresses her own resentment through her narration in *When Dreams Travel.* Rejecting the time frame of the source-text, she reconsiders and reconstructs those days through the eyes of Dunyazad and brings out into the open those elements, which lie hidden in the interstices of the earlier story.

Hariharan also protests against the silencing of the consummate artist Shaharzada after she succeeds in curing the blood-thirsty mindset of the Sultan. The readers are made conscious about the extreme unfairness and injustice of forcing this quick-witted talented woman back to petty domesticity. A woman like Shaharzada, who with her felicitous tongue and innovative spirit saved an entire city is reduced to just another queen in the Sultan's harem. Can she accept it happily after gaining such honour, love and respect from the country as a saviour? Will her talents, remaining imprisoned within the walls of the palace-dungeon, become rusty and useless without being manifested in other spheres? Can she lead a static, commonplace, uneventful life witnessing the harem filling up again with queens and slave-girls? Hariharan feels that after Shaharzada redeemed herself and the women of the land and fell silent her creations, even Dunyazad and Shahzaman, playing the supporting roles, felt torn apart and orphaned. So, what might have been the mental state of the artist herself? Hariharan puts up these questions in her novel *When Dreams Travel* after reading between the lines of the famous legend. She highlights the creativity of the female storyteller who has been totally ignored by the blunt, insensitive, comfortable male assumptions. So, our author, as if a descendant of this legendary storyteller queen, takes it upon herself to reconstruct stories about these narrators, listeners and the people around them.

Hariharan revives certain silent characters from the legend, revitalizes them and also creates new faces in her novel, which is a major departure from the source text. Throughout the legend, Dunyazad is silent except occasionally rousing the interest of the Sultan by questioning her sister. We see her always as an attendant accomplice of her sister. She has no other definite purpose or role to play. But Dunyazad is the heroine of Hariharan's *When Dreams Travel.* She is the major character of the novel in whose consciousness, the past, present and future converge to release a bout of intertextual creativity. In this way she resurrects the past but in a completely different vein from that of the legend. We come to know how the tales were told in response to the request of this mute witness to Shaharzada's thousand and one nights. Also a virgin, she too had offered herself as a martyr instead of Shaharzada. The two sisters even thought how to get rid of the oppressive monarch once an heir was born. Dunyazad's frustrations and agony comes out when she looks back at herself always acting as an attendant, dressing according to other's wishes and never being able to assert her own free will. So, she screams out in anger and grief, not finding any trace of her name on her sister's tomb, even in her dream. Dunyazad also suffered and sacrificed much for a thousand and one nights like her elder sister. She too had no life of her own but to remain awake for so many long continuous nights outside the royal bed-chamber. And after witnessing the fulfilment of the Sultan's bodily urge through the moanings and groanings of the couple, it was her duty to make her sister tell interesting stories to beguile the Sultan. So along with Shaharzada, Dunyazad too deserves a reward in redeeming the kingdom and all women. But with faint resentment she remembers how her sister Shaharzada always occupied the centre stage leaving her aside. Hariharan in her novel focuses on the experiences and aspirations of this ignored Dunyazad after a long period of time. She journeys to the old palace to find out how her sister died so suddenly. We also come to know from her story how the once ruthless Sultan was imprisoned by his son Umar in the magnificent mausoleum, supposedly built for Shaharzada.

Through Dunyazad's recollections of her childhood days, Hariharan beautifully portrays the character of Raziya, the Wazir's wife and the proud mother of two beautiful daughters. But that is not all. The legend does not require her for flaunting the tales of male adventures. Or even if she is mentioned, her role is limited to being a suppressed wife and a voiceless mother. But our author, through the vision of Dunyazad, sees Raziya as a thoughtful, sensitive human being capable of independent wishes and desires, though unable to voice them. As a mother she too has a right to take decisions about the lives of her daughters and is enraged at heart at being denied the right. Her silent death is her protest against the injustice meted out upon her daughters.

Thus the silenced and absenced 'mother' hidden behind the colourful stories of the legend is conferred visibility and audibility here. Hariharan also brings to limelight characters like Dilshad and Sahiba, the slave-girl and the nursemaid of the palace who were always behind the curtain in the source text. Dunyazad's encounter with them in the old palace after a gap of so many years brings out their feelings and personalities. Dunyazad's attachment to Dilshad, their telling of stories to each other brings out many hidden facts and suppressed feelings of many characters of the legend. They re-enact and revive Shaharzada, whose tongue had saved her life. Again Dilshad's tales of flight and fancy bring alive

Satyasama, the freakish poet whose tongue had caused her so much misery.

The character of Satyasama is purely an invention of Hariharan in *When Dreams Travel.* We do not find her anywhere in the legend. Through this strange character of peculiar habits, Githa Hariharan directly attacks the male-dominated society, which cannot accept that a woman should ever bypass her male counterparts in talent or even in speaking the truth. Woman is always taken to be below the standard who cannot be raised to any respectable position of fame and fortune. So, the tale told by the old woman about 'Rupavati' in Dilshad's story is snarled at by her old husband:

> 'Facts,' he snarled at the old woman. 'You have all your facts wrong. How dare you pollute this house with such unrealistic lies? Listen—and correct yourself before it's too late.' (181)

The old man subverts it to 'Rupavata,' a beautiful man. But when the poet-woman Satyasama turns the story inside out, she is whisked and kicked out of the house by the aged couple.

Githa Hariharan also goes on shifting and interchanging the roles of narrators and addressee, thus carving out amazing feats of departure from the source text. She unfolds a series of parings which alternately tells stories in the two parts of the novel. In the first part, two brothers Shahryar and Shahzaman and two sisters Shaharzada and Dunyazad—four characters are in the embrace of the night. Shaharzada is the storyteller and the others are her attentive listeners. In the second part of the novel, we see four women. Two pairs—Dilshad and Dunyazad and Shaharzada and Satyasama—(the spirits or jinns), are again in the embrace of darkness. Here the narrators are alternately Dunyazad, the aged widow queen of Samarkhand and the wily slave-girl Dilshad. Their stories mirror those of the earlier ones. These two narrators speak a text that only a woman can write when there is no Sultan in the room to listen or to chop off their heads. They dream their futures and reinvent their lives by ruminating their past. Their power of utterance can also create and re-create legends, history, fantasy, religion, poetry and everything else which exist in this world. Shaharzada's tales made her a saviour and a martyr. She too lives on in the stories of wronged women, told by Dunyazad. Within the stories also these types of pairing and coupling recur revealing the most unexpected coupling at the end of the novel. Once Hariharan creates a situation where Dilshad plays the role of Dunyazad, Dunyazad acts as her rival, the elder sister Shaharzada to the same but now aged Sultan Shahryar. Here we see a surprising departure from *The Arabian Nights* as the Sultan is asked to tell a story.

Shaharzada's act of storytelling in this novel is an act of compulsion as that is the only possible redemption in her situation. Like her compulsive biological procreation, she is forced to accept the task of telling interesting stories. But Hariharan also pinpoints through her feminist insight that Shaharzada's creativity—though compulsive—is her power and her only happiness. It is a desperate struggle of an imprisoned genius to channelise her creativity. In the legend, this creative genius tells obscene stories of male chauvinism. But the saviour queen of *When Dreams Travel* carries the work of 'ecriture feminine' through WL or 'Woman's language' in her stories. This mark of feminine ecriture is also extended in the dreams and mirrors of Dilshad and Dunyazad. The author also tells about the children of Shahryar and Shaharzada and their births during those storytelling nights. Whereas the legend evades such issues, Hariharan brings out the practical and realistic consequences which are bound to occur when a man and woman lead a conjugal life night after night. Again she brings out the pain and anxiety of the woman who wants to give birth to her baby during the day so that she can be present before the Sultan at the scheduled hours of the night. Hariharan wonders how could a woman with all her natural, physical problems and complications act as a new bride for a continuous thousand and one nights, conforting the Sultan both physically and mentally!

The legend concluded with a satisfying completeness. And there Shaharzada's stories were narrated with an unbroken linearity. The basic structure of *The Thousand and One Nights* is an infinite repetitive sequence. But Hariharan foists her narrative on a broken, interrupted structure both in the frame-story as well as in the stories within stories. The narrators of

When Dreams Travel tell each other absurd tales of magic realism which are not always complete leaving the listener perpetually dissatisfied and thirsty for the knowledge of 'What then?.' In the legend, Shaharzada always resumed a new story she had started the previous night but each individual story were autonomous having distinct clear story outlines. But *When Dreams Travel* deals with non-realistic tales with no linear narration. Rather the stories are like logicless dreams traveling in a circuitous mode, interpolated and fragmented like interior monologue. Hariharan however continuously interweaves and intersects (criss-crosses between) the source text and her novel, reminding the reader always about the doubly fictional quality of her novel.

Thus Githa Hariharan succeeds in rendering a shocking conclusion after going through abrupt turns and twists of narration. In the face of the assured happiness promised at the conclusion of the legend, she voices her rejection of the same by leaving her novel open-ended with feelings of vague fears, forebodings and uncertainties. She does not come to any conclusion at the end of *When Dreams Travel.* Rather Hariharan tries to fathom the nucleus of the existence of the storytellers from the perspective of woman writer.

WORKS CITED

Tales From 1001 Arabian Nights (Selected from the original sixteen volumes of the book of *The Thousand Nights and a Night*). Trans. Sir Richard F. Burton. 7th ed. Mumbai, Delhi: Jaico Publishing House, 1999.

Hariharan, Githa. *When Dreams Travel.* London: Picador, 1999.

Kagal, Carmen. "Fantasy Unlimited." Rev of *When Dreams Travel. Indian Review of Books.* Vol. 8, No. 6, 16 March-15 April, 1999.

Kundu, R. "'*For a Story of My* Own'—The Female Quest for Identity: A Global Perspective" in *Feminist English Literature* (Ed. M.K. Bhatnagar). New Delhi: Atlantic Publishers and Distributors, 1999.

——. "Githa Hariharan: Intertext, Metafiction and 'Her Story'" in *Post Independence Indian English Fiction* (Eds. R. Mittapalli and Alessandro Monti), New Delhi: Atlantic Publishers and Distributors, 2001.

Menon, Ritu. "Awake and Dreaming." Rev of *When Dreams Travel. The Book Review.* Vol. 23, No. 1&2, Jan.-Feb., 1999.

12

BOND WITHOUT BONDAGE: BHARATI MUKHERJEE AND JHUMPA LAHIRI

JAYDEEP SARANGI

> But there is neither East nor West,
> Border, nor Breed, nor Birth
> When two strong men stand face to face,
> Though they come from the end of the earth.
>
> —Rudyard Kipling[1]

When Kipling says, "never the twain shall meet," it does not preclude the possibility of meaningful meeting. He is aware of the fact that meaningful meetings need "strong men." Who are these "strong men"? Certainly, those who are not crippled by the burden of their own cultures. Since culture is a human product like any other product, it is subject to flux. Love of one's own culture necessarily does not make one antagonistic toward the alien culture. Chaman Nahal in his article "Cross-cultural Tensions: E.M. Forster and Ruth Jhabvala" says:

> May be two large segments of cultures such as the East and the West cannot meet in harmony; some of us believe they can. All right, they meet in disharmony. It is all the same a meeting, a meeting of meanings. (85-86)

True culture has been defined as the ability to appreciate the other culture. Montague claims, "While this particular ability has many sources, it is generally derived from varied, sympathetic and understanding contacts between people who differ from each other in some respects" (96). Mankind is not a homogeneous mass of living beings. People perceive the world through the "paradigmatic lenses of our culture" (Philip

70). Like biological changes cultural contacts "require adaptation for survival and development" (Harris 350). The nature of the cross-cultural conflicts, confrontations and alliances portrayed in the works of Bharati Mukherjee and Jhumpa Lahiri can be investigated in this context, in terms of available socio-psychological and culture-shock theories.

Cultural crossovers pave way for a hybrid culture and a new process of cultural assimilation. A mixed cultural milieu makes room for vistas of communication and dialogue in this cosmopolitan world. As an outcome, diasporic reciprocation has become one of the recurrent themes in post-colonial literature. Expatriation often works both as metaphor for physical displacement and as a socio-psychological identity question. The writings of Bharati Mukherjee bear the stamp of the rootlessness caused by Diaspora. The Canadian mosaic of the cultural trends give her a unique form of multiculturalism. After becoming a U.S. citizen in 1988, looking back at her days in Canada (1966-1980), Bharati Mukherjee recognizes herself as an expatriate there who had clung to her ethnic associations. She defends her multicultural identity in *The New York Times Book Review* (1998):

> I was a psychological expatriate though a naturalized Canadian for fifteen years simply because Canada is a country officially hostile to the concept of assimilation. Perceiving myself to be in a comfortable but unwelcoming environment, I struggled to maintain various emblems of my difference.

In the collection of short stories entitled *Darkness* (1985) four are written in Canada. They are "The World according to Hsu," "Isolated Incidents," "Hindus" and "Courtly Vision." According to Bharati Mukherjee, "they are uneasy stories about expatriation."[2] "In the World according to Hsu," Ratna, an Indian origin, and her Canadian husband Graeme Clayton, Professor of Psychology at McGill University, are on holiday at an island of Africa. Graeme Clayton tries to persuade Ratna to move from French dominant Montreal to English dominant Toronto. Ratna prefers to stay back in Montreal for her fascination for the English identity. Graeme reads an article in *The Scientific American* during his stay in Africa. The article deals with cultural collision and separation. The story of "In the World according to Hsu" is written from the expatriate's point of view. "Isolated Incidents" is an account of the native Canadian Anne Vane. Anne Vane's assignment is to file complaints from immigrants on violation of Human Rights. Two interesting cases of racial discrimination in Canadian city of Toronto are brought to her notice. She is aware of the possible result of such cases. "Hindu" reveals the basic dilemma of the immigrants. Leela Lahiri, a Bengali Brahmin origin, finds her bond with America: "I am an American citizen" (133). She also discovers her longing for her Bengali root. Bharati Mukherjee's multi-dimensional characters do not share any hostile distancing from their homeland. They even do not neglect the call of the alien identity. The rigid concept of irreconcilable hostility thus seems to be receding in favour of an evolving consciousness of coexistence. Bharati Mukherjee works for a fruitful outcome from cross-cultural interactions. Her movement from Canada to the United States, she says, in the "Introduction" to the collection of her short stories entitled *Darkness* "is a movement away from aloofness of expatriation to the exuberance of immigration" (3). In *Jasmine* (1990), Bharati Mukherjee celebrates the fluid identities of the protagonist. Bharati Mukherjee observes Calcutta and Indian mores from the typical western's point of view. There are constant attempts to make a bridge between ignorance and affluent or alliances and cross-cultural differences. Cross-cultural transaction is an interactive, dialogic, two-way process rather than a simple active-passive relation. Bharati Mukherjee's characters with different socio-cultural experiences relate to a process involving complex negotiation and exchange.

Jhumpa Lahiri's *Interpreter of Maladies,*[3] a collection of short stories, offers the reader a variety of experiences that are both familiar and alien—all concern Indian protagonists living either in Indian soil or in the United States. A culture within its ambit works as a unifying factor whereas across nations, as a dividing factor. It is natural that an individual gradually comes to terms with an alien culture, despite his/her initial problems of adjustment. From his/her first culture contact in the process of assimilation, four stages of development are registered: The tourist phase, the culture-shock phase, the conformist phase and the assimilation phase (Torbiorn 1982: 90-93). Jhumpa Lahiri is caught between the socio-cultural nuances of her Indian origin and the American life-ways. In an interview she says, "It [America] is home to me but [I] feel a bit of an outsider too."[4] Like her characters, Jhumpa Lahiri undergoes the culture-shock syndrome. It includes four chronological psychosomatic developments. First is the honeymoon stage—the initial admiration for the foreign culture. Then is the crisis phase—where one discovers the socio-cultural and socio-linguistic differences. In this stage one suffers from a sense of anxiety and loss. The next is the recovery stage, when the paradox is resolved. In this phase, one tries to pick up alien conventions, including cultural and linguistic behaviour. The last stage is that of adjustment. In this phase one tries to overcome the preliminary shock of alien culture.

After Arundhati Roy's Booker for *The God of Small Things*, Jhumpa Lahiri becomes the first South Asian to win an individual Pulitzer for the year 2000. We strongly feel that without the biographical details of Lahiri no article is complete. She was born in 1967 in London to Bengali parents who emigrated from Calcutta (now Kolkata), the Capital city of West Bengal, and was raised in Rhode Island, USA. Therefore, Lahiri had the experience of three continents. In the Third and finial Continent, Jhumpa Lahiri indirectly speaks of her multicultural (rootless?) identity through the mouth of an unidentifiable 'I' who seems to be the narrator as well as an active participant in the dialogue format of the last chapter of the book:

> Whenever he is discouraged, I tell him that if I can survive on three continents, then there is no obstacle he cannot conquer, while the astronauts, heroes forever, spent more hours on the moon, I have remained in this new world for nearly thirty years. (197-98)

The author-narrator does not stop at this point. She goes even further:

> I am not the only man to seek his fortune far from home, and certainly I am not the first. Still, there are times I am bewildered by each mile I have traveled, each meal I have eaten, each person I have known, each room in which I have slept. (198)

Jhumpa Lahiri claims that her stories in *Interpreter of Maladies* are "stories of Bengal, Boston and beyond." The stories reflect the multiple identity of the author-narrator. Her yearning for the Indian sensibility (as that is her root) bears the stamp of a vagrant searching for her lost home. She is as if in self-exile. Jhumpa's Indian characters and the Indian sensibility is not all misfit in the American permissive society. She sincerely accepts the problems of setting somewhere else far from the native land:

> I have spent many months with Relatives here and learnt about my parents' home and where they lived. I have always felt integrated with the place [...]. My parents never felt at home. Being the child of immigrants I did not feel at home too. It's taken a long time for me as feel at home anywhere [...].[5]

Feeling at home can be an indication of a process, which is known as adaptation. Man cannot be uprooted thoroughly from his socio-cultural fixity. Yet, none can transcend his cultural identity; certainly no great writer like Jhumpa Lahiri does. *Interpreter of maladies* with sub title "Stories of Bengal, Boston and beyond" projects the problems of the immigrants under the alien sky, the yearning of exile, the emotional confusion.

Jhumpa Lahiri can be grouped with Salman Rushdie or Bharati Mukherjee for her status as 'migrant' writer. The migrant writers project their identity as plural and partial. 'Migrancy' and the 'vagrancy' give birth to the question of crisis of identity. Jhumpa can never have the sense of belongingness. She feels as if she is cut off from the main stream. Her mind yearns for her 'Imaginary homeland.' This is undoubtedly a common scene in the green-card holding Indian diaspora. The writers of this genre are in a fix. In *Interpreter of Maladies* six of the nine stories are set in America, but deal with the lives of Indian immigrants—the Indians in USA. These immigrants live in America but they still belong to their 'home' community. These people are caught between the strict traditions they've inherited and the baffling New World they must encounter everyday. The other three stories are set in India.

The opening story "A Temporary Matter" portrays an ontological condition dealing with the conjugal crisis of a young couple—Shoba and Shukumar. The decline of their mutual attachment in Boston prepares the readers for the problems of self-exile. Memories of India come again in their intimate conversation:

> "It's like India," Shoba said, watching him tend his makeshift candelabra. "Sometimes the current disappears for hours at a stretch. I once had to attend an entire rice ceremony in the dark. The baby just cried and cried. It must have been so hot." (11)

This story is an in-depth study of human psychology. The Americanized Bengali couple exhibits the trends of typical post-colonial diaspora where the characters carry different socio-geographical identities with them. India is discussed in a foreign soil. These trans-cultural references give an advantage to Jhumpa to have wide range of readers.

The second story is set again in Boston. The readers are introduced to Mr Pirzada. He is from Dacca, "the capital of Bangladesh, but then a part of Pakistan" (23). The story has the civil war in Pakistan as well as the birth of Bangladesh as a free state (in 1971) as the backdrop. Mr Pirzada befriends a Bengali family in Boston. He seemed to be disturbed as his family stayed Dacca. Later in the story, he was reunited with his family:

> He was reunited, he wrote, with his wife and children. All were well, having survived the events of the past year at an estate belonging to his wife's grandparents in the mountains of Shillong. (41-42)

"Interpreter of Maladies," the title story, is set in Puri, India. The readers are introduced to Mr Das and Mrs Das. There is an elaborate description of the Sun Temple of Konarak, Orissa. They visit the great Sun Temple in an "ideal weather for sightseeing." Jhumpa, like a veteran craftsman describes the dress of the family:

> The family looked Indian but dressed as foreigners did, the children in stiff, brightly colored clothing and caps with translucent visors. (44)

Jhumpa presents the family as if they are of mixed/hybrid cultures. In language, Jhumpa follows the American tradition of spellings favouring 'colour' to 'colour.' Interestingly, she makes use of Indian words/phrases *'Astachala-Surya'* (setting sun), *'hanuman'* (monkey), *'Nagamithunas'* (act of sex), *'villa'* (place).

Jhumpa Lahiri is careful in her details. There is reference to paperback tour book "India." More interestingly the book has been published abroad. "India" which is about real India must have been published from India. Jhumpa does not want the book to be published in India. She does so to add more dimensions into it.

In this complex story of an Indian American couple Mr Kapasi, a tour-guide and chauffeur plays an important role. Mrs Das discloses the real identity of Bobby to Kapasi. We come to know that a Punjabi-Indian friend of her husband is his father.

A 'most obvious question' gets to the 'heart of the matter' and Mr Kapasi asks, "Is it really pain you feel, Mrs Das, or is it guilt?" Mr Kapasi, the interpreter of people's maladies, fails to offer any remedy to Mrs Das's malady. A multiple identity may be a reason for Mrs Das's queer sexual behaviour. In this context, we cannot reject her cultural uprootedness.

"A real Durwan" begins with Boori ma, 'sweeper of the stairwell' of a multistoried building. Her services "come to resemble those of real durwan" (73). The streets and place names of Calcutta are mentioned here and there in this story of boori ma. 'College Street,' 'Circular Road,' 'Jodhpur Park,' 'Howrah Bridge' add realistic appeal to the story. The vagaries of material possession plaguing human relationship forms the matrix of this story. The story is based on "search for a real durwan."

"Sexy," the fifth story of this collection depicts Miranda, a young energetic American who falls in love with Dev, a married Bengali banker. Dev's wife is away for some days. This story again highlights weak conjugal tics. And we are stuck in the basic 'out of sight out of mind.' Miranda and Dev develop references to breaking of commitment in the husband-wife relationship again and again in the story. They float in the airy nothing as if they have no real root anywhere.

Mrs Sen, in the story named after her, has a distinctive as well as individualistic speech: "Every one, this people, too much in their world"—her impression of America. Her evocation of homeland is convincing and extremely enjoyable:

> She had brought the blade from India, where apparently there was at least one in every household. "Whenever there is a wedding in the family," she told Eliot one day, "or a large celebration of any kind, my mother sends out word in the evening for all the neighbourhood women to bring blades just like this one, and then they sit in an enormous circle on the roof of our building, laughing and gossiping and slicing fifty kilos of vegetables through the night." (115)

Simple household activities in India are mentioned in this story with accuracy. Mrs Sen wants the job for an engagement to fill up her loneliness in afternoons. There is reference to the people of Kolkata for their keen interest for fish: "in Calcutta people ate fish first thing in the morning, last thing before bed, as a snack after school if they were lucky" (123).

This story projects the difficulties faced by Indian wives in a foreign culture. A sense of alienation pre-occupies the hearts of people culturally as well as geographically cut off from their homeland. A sense of loss runs all through the story: "Do you miss your mother, Eliot, there afternoons with me?"

> "You must miss her [...]."
> "I see her at night."
> "When I was your age I was without knowing that one day I would be so far [...]." (122-23)

Jhumpa Lahiri, a perfect interpreter of a cultural multiplicity, is faithful enough to project Indian culture and tradition in realistic terms. She portrays Mrs Sen as she is. Jhumpa knows that fish can be palatable and enjoyable for Mrs Sen as she has her root in the Bengali tradition: "The other thing that made Mrs Sen happy was fish from the seaside" (123).

Bibi Haldar, too, in the story, "The Treatment of Bibi Haldar," is presented against an Indian socio-cultural backdrop.

She is about 29 years old. She suffers from "an ailment that baffled family, friends, priests, palmists, spinsters, gem therapists, prophets, and fools" (158). Bibi finally has a miraculous cure. She becomes pregnant. She says, "I'm contagious, like the pox. She says I'll spoil the baby." Later on she delivers a 'forcep' baby. Marriage proves to be a panacea for Bibi. The final authorial remarks confirms Bibi comparatively better health condition: "she was, to the best of our knowledge, cured" (172).

Interpreter of Maladies is a muniments of cultural multiplex, which is multinominal as well. Jhumpa, through her experience of different cultural identities come to know the basic properties of different cultures. The nations are not merely geo-political identities. One who is born and brought up in a cultural situation makes his own root there. When he is planted elsewhere he becomes a member of that culture. But the total adaptation in a new soil is next to impossible. One who is in exile ('self' or 'forced') may find him in the cultural and linguistic crux. Is it cultural multiplicity? Why can't we brand it as cultural uprootedness? One is migrated means he is uprooted societally and psychologically. When it is psychological there must be an inclination for the homeland. And the self is divided. One must fall back to nostalgic past. He may experience an alienation from a stream of life, a tradition and bandage for what he was known for: he is caught between the stools. His identity becomes plural and partial. If plural, he symbolizes cultural multiplicity, and if partial, he stands for cultural uprootedness. Jhumpa Lahiri's stories are perceptive critique of human relationships, bonds and commitments that one has to make with homeland as well as the migrated land. Man in exile has these dual responsibilities to carry out.

The immigrants like Jhumpa Lahiri project two or more cultures to accomplish different, sometimes divergent roles and functions, their distribution in different contexts and geo-political identities. Bi-culturalism or multi-culturalism in whatever way we interpret Jhumpa Lahiri's stories, a socio-cultural criss-cross is there. Her stories establish interpersonal bond without bondage.

Bapsi Sidhwa, an immigrant writer, is often asked, "As a recent migrant how comfortable are you writing about America?" Bapsi Sidhwa has the answer:

> The compulsion to transpose experience into narrative, to convey a personal vision, is what makes one write in the first place. Creating fiction is essentially subjective and my assessment of what is striking in America, and of how my family and I have coped in our new circumstances, are bound to insinuate their way into my writing. (162)

Bapsi Sidhwa confesses the hardships the immigrant writers are bound to be troubled with:

> Of course, it is not easy to portray the nuances of a culture one is not born to, and it entails a risk to get inside the shin of a character that is shaped by another culture.

The immigrant writers are like journeymen who are caught between two or more cultures. The characters of cross-cultural writings are compared to life in the New World (in which they are in) with the ways and values in the native world in which they are more accustomed to.

The chronic uprooting of the immigrant writers as well as the characters demand adjustments that cause tensions. Jhumpa Lahiri's sense of being an outsider runs through the pages. It is shared by her characters:

> Jhumpa Lahiri's elegant stories tell the lives of Indians in exile, of people navigating between the strict traditions they've inherited and the baffling New World they must encounter everyday.[6]

Jhumpa has close approximity with V.S. Naipaul. Naipaul's relationship to India or the Caribbean closely resembles Jhumpa's relationship to India and Rhode Island. Jhumpa's 'Pulitzer prize for fiction 2000' pays gracious tribute to USA and India, the two civilizations which matter to her. The thirst for roots drive Jhumpa and her characters to India. In the process, Jhumpa looks for Indian traditions, cultural heritage, sculpture and the life-way of the Indians. She finds an oblique relation to them. The cross-cultural encounters, as depicted by Bharati Mukherjee and Jhumpa Lahiri, assume that one group (usually the minority in an alien socio-cultural context) is bound to be absorbed by another. People belonging to this minority group modify their behaviour to cope with all sorts of problems they encounter in a foreign country. They tend to establish a (hypothetical) socio-cultural and socio-linguistic bond with the members of the alien society.

NOTES

1. Rudyard Kipling, "The Ballad of East and West," *A Kipling Anthology.* Ed. W.G. Bebbington (London: Methuen & Co., 1964) 66 & 70.
2. Bharati Mukherjee, "Introduction," *Darkness* (Ontario: Penguin, 1986) 2. All subsequent page references are from this edition of the text.
3. The edition I quote from is: Jhumpa Lahiri, *Interpreter of Maladies: Stories of Bengal, Boston, and Beyond* (New Delhi: Harper Collins India, 1999).
4. Jhumpa Lahiri in an interview, http: / /www.rediffmail.com/news/2000/apr/11 jhumpa.htm, P-l.
5. *The Times of India,* Kolkata edition, January 21, 2001.
6. Introductory note of *Interpreter of Maladies.*

WORKS CITED

Harris, Philip R. "Effectiveness with Cultural Differences," *Managing Cultural Differences* (Houston: Gulf Publishing Co., 1979).

Lahiri, Jhumpa. *Interpreter of Maladies* (New Delhi: Harper-Collins India, 1999).

Montague, M.F. Ashley. *Man's Most Dangerous Myth* (New York: Columbia Univ. Press, 1945).

Mukherjee, Bharati. *Darkness* (Ontario: Penguin, 1986).

——. "Immigrant Writing: Give us your Maximalists," *The New York Times Book Review,* August 28, 1998.

Nahal, Chaman. "Cross-cultural Tensions: E.M. Forster and Ruth Jhabvala," *The New Literatures in English* (New Delhi : Allied Publishers, 1985).

Philip, P.J. "Emerging Issues in Cultural Relations in an Independent World," *Topics in Culture Learning 4* (1976).

Sidhwa, Bapsi. "Writing as an Immigrant" (New Delhi: *ALR,* Oct.-Dec. 2000) 162.

Torbiorn, Ingemar. "Culture Shock and the U-shaped Adjustment Curve," *Living Abroad* (New Delhi: Wiley & Sons, 1982) 90-93.

13

THE 'NEW WOMAN' IN POST-INDEPENDENCE NOVELS: AN EMERGING IMAGE

SMRITI SINGH

Writing is not an area of activity from which women have been excluded or in which they have failed to gain equality with men. As novelists, Sir Walter Scott and Jane Austen share supremacy. In fact, Scott wrote in his Diary, "Edgeworth, Ferrier, Austen have all given portraits of real society far superior to anything man, vain man, has produced of the like nature."

In India, too, women have been writing novels since the end of the 19th century. What interests us is their portrayal of Indian women in their novels. Another question which draws our attention is whether the Image of the Indian woman has changed with time or has it remained the same. If it has changed, then what is the "new woman" like?

The "New Woman" first appeared in English literature in the novels of the great Victorians. Towards the end of the 19th certury, Grant Allen's *The Women Who Did*, Thomas Hardy's *Tess of the D'urbervilles* and other works favoured a New image of woman. When Hardy sub-titled his novel "a pure woman," he issued a deliberately provocative challenge to conventional notions of purity. A similar movement to propagate New Woman Ideas can be traced in Indian English novels. But there is a Major difference between the new woman of the English tradition and that of Indo-Anglian Novels. Here the woman has to face complex social forces at work. Therefore, the Indian writers have tried to keep within cultural bounds in order to be realistic.

Indian woman has numerous facets. She may be kind, sensitive, intelligent, jealous, patient, protective and overpowering. She is a complex figure, a mystery too deep to understand. Throughout the centuries, she has been identified with the mythical figures of Sita, Savitri, Durga, Lakshmi and Saraswati. The early Indian novels by male writers had idealized and romanticised images of women taken from history. Slowly, writers like Tagore in "Binodini," Premchand in "Sevasadan," "Nirmala," "Gaban," Sarat Chandra in "Shubhadra" started drawing very realistic images from everyday life. Throughout the latter part of the 19th certury and the earlier part of the 20th, one witnesses the writers' increasing preoccupation with the problems of women.

This period also saw the emergence of a number of women writers like Toru Dutt, Krupabai Sathianathan, Mrs. Swarna Kumari Ghosal and Cornelia Sorabjee. Among these early women writers, Shevanti Bai Nikambe is another name of importance. She was a social worker who wrote her novel *Ratnabai* (1895) with the aim of building up public opinion in favour of educating girls. It is, indeed, a matter of shame that what Shevanti Bai was espousing so long ago is still not within the grasp of many Indian women.

Women as rebels were first introduced in the novels dealing with the Independence movement. Women of all ages and from all classes responded to Gandhiji's call for a non-violent struggle against British domination. As the freedom struggle was of major importance, all other issues were relegated to a secondary place in novels dealing with the struggle for independence. In encouraging women to come out of their homes and join the national movement, Gandhiji moved a big step forward from the nineteenth certury reformers, but he, too, had his limitations:

> The role of women in the freedom struggle was supportive and auxiliary, limited to spinning, picketing, distributing literature, and attending meetings. He also found women as symbols of self-sacrifice who should neither be the principal bread-winner in a family nor disrupt the balance at home.[1]

This aspect of Gandhian philosophy is reflected in the novels of the twenties and thirties. Many writers writing during this period were obsessed with political themes and social issues which Gandhiji propagated and those become the main subjects of fiction.

Dr A.V. Krishna Rao comments on the novels written during this time:

> Almost all the Indo-Anglian novels have one or more of the following nuclear ideas predominant in them: the evil of partition; the cult of "Quit India; and the Gandhian myth."[2]

In post-independence Indo-Anglian novels, there is a marked shift from the emphasis on the life of the community and the nation, to the portrayal of the inner life of the individual. All conflicts and tensions of modern life are seen in the light of their effect on a sensitive, educated Indian:

> One might say that in spite of the fact that some Indo-Anglian novelists are still attempting to recapture a recent historical part, the majority of writers since 1950 have turned inwards to more private and personal concerns.[3]

And in post-independence Indian novels, many writers have made the modern Indian woman the protagonist of their novels. Sometimes, the novelist used the image of a frustrated woman as a symbol of the seething discontent raging within the heart of any ordinary Indian. At other times, the artist's own insecurity and sense of isolation in a changing world found a mirror in the woman's consciousness. This was especially the case with novels written by women writers. These dark corners of the female psyche that had remained veiled all these years came under purview. One of the most pressing problems confronted by the Indian woman in modern India is the desire to find self-fulfilment while conforming to the values of the past. How to conform? How much to break away to assert one's individuality? This inner struggle to find a balance between tradition and modernity has been portrayed more authentically by the women writers, than by men. One reason for a sketchy protrayal by men is that they hardly had any opportunity to study the female sex. The Indian women were kept strictly segregated even from the men in their own family. They had separate living quarters. So girls tended to become symbols as in the novels of Raja Rao or were projected as objects of pity, silent and suffering, as in the works of Mulk Raj Anand. Sohini in *Untouchable* is a meek, patient and courageous sufferer and the same can be said about Laila in *Two Leaves and a Bud.* Though R.K. Narayan has a variety of women figures—wives, mothers, grandmothers and aunts—they do not even possess a name. These faceless women playing their pre-ordained roles endure hardships and accept all misfortunes with a stoic resilience. By their very anonymity and facelessness, R.K. Narayan has succeeded in conveying the predicament of the Indian woman in a middle class family.

A comparison between the early women novelists and the later women novelists of the post-independence era shows a definite continuity in trend and approach. In both the periods, women characters have been shown to be searching for identity, for self-awareness. In the earlier novels, women rebelled against major social issues like child marriage, denial of education to girls, and atrocities suffered by a woman in her husband's house. In contemporary novels, there is more depth and complexity in the choice and treatment of women. Just as modern society is complex, so are the women. The modern novels have women who rebel against accepting the traditional feminine roles. They have challenged the accepted ideals of marriage and maternity, and have chosen to work for a living instead. They refuse to conform to the image of the effeminate, docile, silent and long suffering woman, a picture invented and nurtured through a male oriented culture. The women of contemporary fiction are revolutionary in nature and the emphasis is on creating a totally new character type. The new woman in Indian fiction is talented, intelligent, and indulges in deep self-analyses and introspection. She has refused to accept unquestioningly the rules fixed for her by an ancient outmoded culture.

The majority of women in the earlier novels are shown to suffer the external forces of economic hardships, natural calamities, like flood and famines. From among the women novelists of the 1950s, Kamala Markandaya has a varied repertoire of women characters in her fiction. Her novels contain figures who show patience and forebearance under extremely tortuous circumstances. Ira, the sweet, obedient and hard-working daughter of Nathan in *Nectar in a Sieve* (1954) is one such example. Rejected by her husband for her barrenness, she showers her love and care on her younger brother. During the famine, she starves herself to feed him. When that too proves insufficient, she sells her body. Rukmani, her mother is also the very model of a typical Indian wife intensely devoted to her husband. Even when she hears about his infidelity, she remains silent. While *Nectar in a Sieve* is about a peasant woman and her fight for survival, *A Handful of Rice* (1966) is about the plight of the urban poor. Both Rukmani and Nalini win the reader's sympathy for their courage in facing great odds. Tension in marriage and the effect it has on the woman-man relationship is dealt with in *A Silence of Desire* (1961) while *Possession* (1963) and *The Nowhere Man* (1972) deal with the problems women face due to cultural differences between East and West. This cultural conflict forms the backdrop for the conjugal rifts and disharmony in *Some Inner Fury* (1955).

About the female figures of Kamala Markandaya, S. Krishnaswamy says, "In all her novels the author sets forth an inspiring goal-autonomy for the self, nurturance for the family, and fellow feeling for the community of men and women."[4] However, most of her women are so burdened by the problems of everyday life, that they do not have the time to think about independence. She has generally led her heroines to find solace in the old maxims of love, pity, pride, compassion and sacrifice. Those who stray beyond these well traversed ways suffer are meet tragic ends, like Lalitha of "Two Virgins" (1975).

Compared with Kamala Markandaya, Anita Desai is a very different sort of writer, both in her choice and treatment of themes. Her novels contain figures suffering more from the battles raging within them than from outside influences. The central stage, in her novels, is occupied by the unhappy, unfulfilled "mad" woman who tries to resolve the battles raging within her. Anita Desai portrays a woman's inner world, her sensibility and frustrations. Her characters strive to find a balance between the yearnings of their inner self for emancipation and dignity and the outer world which seems insensitive to their problems. Maya in *Cry, the Peacock,* Monisha in *Voices in the City,* Sita in *Where Shall We Go This Summer*—suffer because they find themselves unsuited to play the traditional female's role. Shanta Krishnaswamy writes:

> What she protrays is the deeply felt and suffered rebellion against the entire system of social relationships. The passive feminine has ceased to exist.[5]

Faced with a hostile environment, these sensitive females react and earn the label of insanity.

Maya's unhappiness in *Cry, the Peacock* is the craving of a tortured mind for compassion and understanding. But Gautam, her husband offers her logic and wisdom and is impervious to her suffering. In *Voices in the City* the protagonist Monisha, has a servile existence within the confines of a traditional Hindu family. She learns to block her feelings. Her husband, Jiban is even more insensitive and de-humanized than Gautam and no amount of pain can move him. Monisha, with her stigma of childlessness and her world confined to the barred room within the prison of the joint family, has no means of escape. In the end, the choice left open to her is either that of an unbearable existence or of death. She chooses the latter. She wanted privacy, solitude, a deeper meaning in life but her life was a repetition of monotonous activity, akin to that led by generations of women:

> [...] hidden behind the barred windows of hall-dark rooms, spending centuries in washing clothes, kneading dough and murmuring aloud verses from the Bhagvad-Gita and the Ramayan, in the dim light of sooty lamps. Lives spent in waiting for nothing, waiting on men self-centred and indifferent and hungry and demanding and critical: Waiting for death and dying misunderstood, always behind bars.[6]

Like the detachment of Monisha in *Voice in the City,* and that of Maya in *Cry, the Peacock,* Sita in *Where Shall We Go this Summer* runs away to Manori and thus, rejects the life she is forced to live. Her escape to Manori is, in fact, a search for a deeper meaning to life:

gentleness, forgetting oneself. The ability to succeed in the path without masochism and without annihilating one's affective, intellectual and professional personality—such would seem to be the stakes won through guiltless maternity."[16]

In this novel, the narrative voice fluctuates between the first and the third person; 'she' and 'I' are two facets of the same self. Such shifts express the position of women in a patriarchal society—someone without a clear sense of purpose and without a firm sense of her own dirtity.

Sarita is like the female voice, she does not place herself in the centre of a universe of her own making, but is always aware of the demands and needs of others.

Earlier mothers served as models for their daughters. But in the *Dark Holds No Terrors*, Sarita's mother dies just before the narrative begins and she says:

> Can't you understand, Baba, that it's because she cursed me that I am like this?[17]

Here we can probably see a desire to kill what Judith Kegar Gardiner in her essay "On female Identity and Writing by Women" has termed the "mother villain," the woman whom the daughter fears she will come to resemble, the woman whose life is without the power and worldly success the daughter seeks, the woman who represents an adherence to customs the daughter wishes to overthrow. This desire to be different from 'the mother' is also seen in Manju Kapoor's *Difficult Daughters* (1998). This is the story of women of three generations—Kasturi, Virmati and Ida and is set in pre-independent India. The whole story of Virmati and Kasturi is narrated by Ida, the daughter of Virmati. She, through the story of her mother, does not merely present the text of feminism, but explores the female psyche without the inhibitions of the male world. Just as Virmati is different from Kasturi—more educated, working, engaged in an illicit relationship with Harish—Ida, too, is different from her mother and this is aptly illustrated by her opening remark:

> The one thing I had wanted was not to be like my mother.[18]

All these writers have made a positive contribution towards understanding the psyche of the modern Indian woman and the trauma she undergoes in playing the varied roles in a changing society. On the one hand, she is expected to be docile, sacrificing, a silent but efficient home-maker. On the other, the realities of life force her to find employment, go out of the house, be strong and face the world. She has to find a balance between her own aspirations, and the demands made upon her by her home, her in-laws, her husband and her children. She is no longer satisfied with being a wife and a mother. Her horizons have widened and so have her tensions and workload. All these pressures are revealed and dealt with in these novels. The obvious solution lies in rebellion but these are some inherent dangers in revolt. The woman has to retain her essential womanliness in her fight for emancipation and equality and each writer has provided her own solutions to these vexed issues. Kamala Markandaya does not favour revolt and highlights the nurturing and caring qualities of a woman and sees the salvation of woman in it. In contrast, both Anita Desai and Nayantara Sahgal favour rebellion against subjugation.

Bharati Mukherjee and Jhabvala, being outsiders, view the issues from a distance and therefore, with detachment. They do not provide solutions but aim rather at pointing out the follies and foibles.

Writers like Veena Paintal or Namita Gokhale have sincere and serious intents but they still have a long way to go. There are other woman writers, like Uma Vasudev (*The Song of Anasuya, Shrela of Sonagarh*) and Shobha De (*Socialite Evenings, Starry Nights, Sisters*) who have used the women in their novels as symbols of sex and in the process, have further domesticated the female. But there are a few Indo-Anglian women writers, like Manorama Moss (*Mulligatawny Soup*), Dina Mehta (*And Some Take a Lover*) and Geeta Mehta (*Karma Cola Raj*) who show signs of emerging as serious novelists.

All these writers have tried to highlight the dilemma of the modern Indian woman. She is depicted as someone who is no longer satisfied with just being a mother and a wife. Her horizons have widened and so have her tensions. The established novelists like Kamala Markandaya, Desai, Sahgal have given revolutionary pictures of the New woman, which do not conform to any traditional code of conduct. These women like Mohan, Usha (*The Golden Honey Comb*), Bim (*Clear Light of Day*), Sonali (*Rich Like Us*), have their own ideas about love and marriage. These women have shattered the myth of weak, clinging, dependent woman but they are not tied with limited feminist perspective which tends to freeze women in reaction against men and family life. There is a large concept of humanity to be found in these works. Though these writers have stopped treating motherhood as a marvel, women as frail creatures and marriage as a career, they do not project hysterical feminist views either. Conjugal love and strong family ties are also viewed as important ingredients for a happy, whole woman. Only the options are now open and free. The woman can choose her way of life.

Thus, the main trend in contemporary novels been to portray woman as she is shorn of all mystery, poetry and romance. She is neither idealized on the lines of Sita, Savitri and Shakuntala nor placed on a pedestal and worshipped as a goddess. She has begun to stir out of her cocoon to ask society a few important but awkward questions. There is intense introspection and analysis within her, as she tries to come to terms with the crisis of being caught in a changing society.

NOTES

1. Dastur, A.J. *Gandhi's Contributions to the Emancipation of Women* (Delhi, 1982) 6.
2. Rao, A.V.K. *The Indo-Anglian Novel and the Changing Tradition* (Delhi, 1972) 140.
3. Mukherjee, M. *Twice-Born Fiction* (Delhi, 1971) 206.
4. Krishnaswamy, S. *The Women in Indian Fiction in English* (Delhi, 1984) 163
5. *Ibid.*, 238.
6. Desai, A. *Voices in the City* (Delhi, 1982) 121
7. Desai, A. *Where Shall We Go This Summer?*
8. Mukherjee, B. *Wife* (Delhi, 1976) 13.
9. Sahgal, N. *Rich Like Us* (London, 1985) 28.
10. Mukherjee, B. *Wife* (Delhi, 1976) 28.
11. *Ibid.*, 30.
12. Jhabvala, R.P. *The Householder* (London, 1960) 68.
13. Paintal, V. *Roshni* (Delhi, 1967) 71.
14. *Ibid.*, 289.

15. Paintal, V. *An Autumn Leaf* (Delhi, 1976) 20-21.
16. Kristeva, J. "Women's Time" (*Signs* 7, 1981) 13-35.
17. Deshpande, S. *The Dark Holds No Terrors* (New Delhi: Penguin Books India [P] Ltd., 1990) 197.
18. Kapoor, M. *Difficult Daughters* (New Delhi: Penguin Books India [P] Ltd., 1998) 1.

REFERENCES

Novels

Anand, M.R. *Untouchable*. Bombay: Kutub Popular, 1935.

——. *Two Leaves and a Bud*. rpt. Bombay: Kutub Popular, 1951.

Desai, Anita. *Cry, the Peacock*. (1963) rpt. Delhi: Orient Paperbacks, 1983.

——. *Voices in the City*. (1965) rpt. Delhi: Orient Paperbacks, 1983.

——. *Clear Light of Day*. Delhi: Allied Publishers, 1980.

——. *Where Shall We Go This Summer?* (1975) rpt. Delhi: Orient Paperbacks, 1982.

De, Shobha. *Socialite Evenings*. Delhi: Penguin Books, 1989.

——. *Starry Nights*. Delhi: Penguin Books, 1991.

——. *Sisters*. Delhi: Penguin Books, 1982.

Deshpande, Shashi. *The Dark Holds No Terrors*. New Delhi: Penguin Books India Ltd., 1990.

Jhabvala, R.P. *To Whom She Will*. London: George Allen and Unwin Ltd., 1955.

——. *A Backward Place*. Delhi: Mind Pocket Books, 1965.

——. *Get Ready for Battle*. London: John Murray, 1962.

——. *The Householder*. (1968) rpt. London: Penguin Books, 1980.

——. *Esmond in India*. (1958) rpt. Great Britain: Penguin Books, 1 983.

Kapoor, Manju. *Difficult Daughters*. New Delhi: Penguin Books India (P) Ltd., 1998.

Markandaya, Kamala. *Nectar in a Sieve*. (1955) rpt. Bombay: Jaico Publishing, 1983.

——. *Some Inner Fury*. (1956) Bombay: Jaico Publishing, 1957.

——. *A Silence of Desire*. London: Putnam, 1960.

——. *A Handful of Rice*. Delhi: Orient Paperbacks, 1966.

——. *Two Virgins*. rpt. Delhi: Vikas Publishing House, Pvt. Ltd., 1983.

——. *The Golden Honey Comb*. New York: Thomas Y. Crowell Company, 1977.

——. *Possession*. London: Putnam, 1963.

——. *The Nowhere Man*. Bombay: Sargam Books, 1975.

Mehta, Dina. *And Some Take A Lover*. Delhi: Rupa and Company, 1992.

Mehta, Gita. *Karma Cola.* (1979) rpt. U.S.: Ballartine Books, 1991.

——. *Raj.* NY: Jonathan Cape, 1989.

Moss Manorama. *Mulligatawny Soup.* Delhi: Penguin Publishers, 1983.

Mukherjee, B. *The Tiger's Daughter.* London: Chatto and Windus, 1973.

——. *Wife.* Delhi: Sterling Publishers Pvt. Ltd., 1976.

Paintal, Veena. *Roshini/Serenity in Storm.* Delhi: Mind Pocket-Books, 1967.

——. *An Autumn Leaf.* Delhi: Mind Pocket Books, 1967.

Premchand, M. *Godan Translated by Jac Ratan.* Delhi: Jaico Publishing, 1986.

Sahgal, Nayantara. *This Time of Morning.* Delhi: Hind Pocket Books, 1965.

——. *A Time to be Happy.* Delhi: Heinemann Educational Books Ltd., 1971.

——. *Storm in Chandigarh.* London: Chatto and Windus Ltd., 1969.

——. *The Day in Shadow.* rpt. Delhi: Vikas Publishlng, 1976.

——. *Rich Like Us.* London: William Heinemann Ltd., 1987.

Vasudeva, Uma. *The Song of Anasuya.* Delhi: Vikas Publishing, 1978.

——. *Shreya of Sonagarh.* Delhi: UBS Publishers, 1993.

14

POLYPHONIC VOICES OF INDIAN FEMINISM

SHYAM S. AGARWALLA

Partha Chatterjee foregrounds the subjugation of Indian women thus:

> Colonial critics invariably repeated a long list of atrocities, perpetrated on Indian women, not so much by men or certain classes of men, as by an entire body of scriptural canons and ritual practices which, they said, by rationalising such atrocities within a complex framework of religious doctrine, made them appear to perpetrators and sufferers alike as the necessary marks of right conduct. By assuming a position of sympathy with the unfree and oppressed womanhood of India, the colonial mind was able to transform this figure of the Indian woman to the sign of the inherently oppressive and unfree nature of the entire cultural tradition of the country.[1]

Himani Bannerji contests Partha Chatterjee:

> It is as though there was no patriarchal oppression of women in India, but rather only a colonial fiction of such oppression, a tendentious critique of the colonised culture projected with a view to legitimate colonisation. At best the question of Indian women's oppression in a patriarchal caste culture is bracketed in favour of vindicating nationalist thought [...]. The issue of patriarchy, therefore, becomes unimportant, or even non-existent, because colonisers draw our attention to it [...]. Under such circumstances any social criticism or demand of reform for Indian women would spell

> submission to colonial discourse. Chatterjee's own decolonisation proposal does not permit any critique of patriarchy in India.[2]

This *genderlect* of Bannerji in 2000 AD, in orchestration with Gail Omvedt, Kamala Viswesaran and Uma Chakravarti and a host of Indian women theorists and creative writers, posits patriarchy as a site of violent episteme, in Hindu social and religious structures. Uma Chakravarti's critique of androcratic society posits women's double subjection—by the male patriarchal community and the colonial state. She speaks of "dual structures of authority" of local caste patriarchy and the "new statutory laws" of the colonial state: "Both structures upheld the authority of the patriarchal family, and its property forms even though they were apparently dissimilar and at times in conflict with each other." I take up for consideration the second point, first, *i.e.*, "new statutory laws" of the colonial state, which had subjected Indian women to them. The interpretative community of Indian women, with few exceptions, lays blame for its "slave-bond" position on the "new statutory law" of the colonial state. On the contrary, Queen Victoria's proclamation of 1858 tells a different story:

> Firmly relying ourselves on the truth of Christianity and acknowledging with gratitude the solace of religion, we disclaim alike the right and the desire to impose our convictions on any of our subjects [...]. We do strictly charge and enjoin all those who may be in authority under us that they abstain from all interference with the religious belief or worship of any of our subjects on pain of our highest displeasure.[3]

Arun P. Mukherjee, an anglophone Professor, comments: "In the name of non-interference, the British government refused to address demands for legislation to put an end to untouchability, child marriage, and dowry, and to promote women's rights, property reform, and so on."[4] Hansa Mehta writes: "He (Maharaja Sayajirao of Baroda) also knew the value of girls' education and a high school for girls was opened in 1906 or 1907 when my sister and I were among the first few students."[5] From the very inception of the Indian National Congress its membership was open to women. At its first session Allan Octavian Hume asked political reformers "of all shades of opinion" never to forget that "unless the elevation of the female element of the nation proceeds *pari passu* (with an equal pace) with their work, all their labour for the political enfranchisement of the country will prove vain."[6] Ten women attended the fourth session of the Congress at Bombay in 1889. Some women writers, though small in numbers, had written some outstanding novels. In *Sultana's Dream*, Rokeya Sakhawat Hossain, in 1905, writes about Sultana. The subversion of the patriarchal order and the colonization is effected craftily by Rokeya. First of all, the men against whom the women employ their intelligence are from the military. "When the women were engaged in scientific researches," writes Sultana, "the men of this country (Ladyland) were busy increasing their military power." 1905 was the year when Rabindranath Tagore wrote his *Home and the World*. Rokeya adroitly posits the Ladyland of her novel in a European country: "Sultana's image of final empowerment is thus not only a release from the first colonization by men, but also the equally dehumanizing one of the British."[7] Uma Chakravarti's *Overcoding* of the patriarchal order and the colonial rule are playful recording of illusory and anxiety-ridden fears of semi-barbaric countries and "Among the Believers."

Gayatri Chakravorty Spivak poses a rhetorical question, "Can the Subaltern Speak?":

> Within the effaced itinerary of the subaltern subject, the track of sexual difference is doubly effected. The question is not of female participation in insurgency, or the ground rules of the sexual division of labour, for both of which there is 'evidence.' It is, rather, that, both as object of colonialist historiography and as subject of insurgency, the ideological construction of gender keeps the male dominant. If, in the context of colonial production, the subaltern has no history and cannot speak, the subaltern as female is even more deeply in shadow [...].[8]

Cixous's *ecriture feminine* speaks of a phallocentric system that she sees as a regulative force in our discourse. Rokeya, Svarna Kumari Devi (the sister of Tagore), Sarojini Naidu, in colonial India, do not fully upstage that system but they, at least, subvert it enough to call for a new narratology—one that will be less "deeply in shadow."

The Hindu canonical texts, like the *Rigveda* the *Upanishads*, the *Valmiki Ramayan*, and the *Mahabharata*, based on the oral culture and narration are like *formulaic literature*, heavily dependent on the memory. John Cawelti has defined a formula as a "combination or synthesis of a number of specific cultural conventions with a more universal story form or archetype."[9] The Hindu canonical texts are, thus, a synthesis or combination of a number of specific cultural conventions, propped up with memory. Edward Said's *Orientalism* claims that the peculiarly "Western style for dominating, restructuring, and having authority over the Orient"[10] is inextricable from the peculiarly Western style of studying and thinking about the Orient. Strictly speaking, "Orientalism" designates the pioneering efforts of eighteenth-century scholars and enthusiasts of Oriental culture—such as William Jones, Henry T. Colebrooke and Charles Wilkins—who undertook the first translations of texts like the *Bhagavad Gita, Shakuntala* and portions of the *Upanishads*. This Orientalist discourse was not only available to colonials but to colonized, also. Gandhian cultural resistance, Richard Fox argues, typically "depended upon an Orientalist image of India as inherently spiritual, consensual, and corporate."[11] Leela Gandhi, an anglophone critic and teacher, writes: "Correspondingly, enthusiastic Indian nationalists responded to pejorative stereotypes about India's caste-dominated, other-worldly, despotic and patriarchal social structure with reformist zeal and agency. Thus, Orientalist discourse was strategically available not only to the empire but also to its antagonists."[12] Tejaswini Niranjana, in her book, *Siting Translation*, writes about William Ward's preface to his three-volume *A View of the History, Literature, and Mythology of the Hindoos*, which "is instructive for the virulence with which it attacks the depravity and immorality of the natives. Their religion, manners, customs, and institutions are shown to be characterized, like those of other pagans, by "impurity" and "cruelty" [...]. The author claims, in his obsessive reference to "native" sexuality, to have witnessed innumerable scenes of "impurity," for the Hindu institutions are "hotbeds of impurity," and the very services in the temples present "temptations to impurity [...] Ward sees the Hindus as corrupt by nature, lacking the means of education and improvement [...]. The strategies of containment initiated by translation are therefore deployed across a range of discourses, allowing us to name translation as significant technology of colonial domination."[13] The Orientalists, as stated above, in their non-essentialist studies of Indian religion, mythologies, scriptures, customs, and traditions, have taken recourse to *meconnaissance*, interpolation, deviation, have foregrounded violence, not in British India, but, in precolonial India. Like Gandhiji, Indian women—theorists and creative writers—have believed the contingent, Eurocentric, views of Hindu scriptures and religion, forgetting that these views were transfused into the body of Hindu scriptures and religion by Orientalists. This is something like Jean Baudrillard's *simulacrum*, a substitute for *representation*. Indian women, writers, critics, social scientists, and political activists, substitute *simulacrum* or *simulation* of the Orientalist for *representation* of a *dispositif* of Hindu scriptures and rituals. Their foreclosure by the Orientalists is understandable but the *fictogram* of Indian women writing is bricolage, of all that is Western, of a trace left by the Orientalists. Indian feminist writers, for instance, have installed Kali, in place of Savitri, Sita, Draupadi and Damayanti, for Kali is a sign of power and destruction. As she annihilates the mighty demon Raktabija by drinking his blood, she epitomizes the destruction of male principle and phallic power. They have also established a publishing house, Kali for Women, in New Delhi. Like the Orientalists, the Indian feminists' foreclosure of other important goddesses, like Saraswati and Laxmi, is the *meconnaissance* of the thermolabile substance of *genderlect*. The Judaic-Christian-Islamic theology presents the Supreme Reality or the Supreme Person as God. In the Hebrew Psalter there is no hymn to a Goddess. The opening words of the Lord's prayer in the Church of England are: "Our Father, which art in heaven," the Exordium of the *Holy Koran* praises Allah as "Lord of the Creation." In the religion known as Hinduism there are both gods and goddesses and the Supreme Person is here conceived as both masculine and feminine. There is also the other question—Is Kali

Dravidian or Aryan? In his book *The Dravidian Element in Indian Culture* (1924), Gilbert Slater identifies Kali with one of the village goddesses described in Bishop H. Whitehead's *Village Gods of Southern India* (2nd ed., 1921). The anger of the Western feminists against patriarchal society cannot be equated with their counterparts in India, for reasons embedded in their theology. Therefore, there is no feminist publishing house, which is called either Diana for Women, Minerva for Women or Cybele for Women. In Hinduism, Kali is worshipped by both male and female. When Bacon said prosperity is the blessing of the *Old Testament*, adversity of the *New* he meant a kind of realism in higher religion where divine grace shines through grief and even terror. It is this realism in spiritual life which makes Ramprasad's Mother raise her hand in benediction in the midst of a calvary littered with human skulls. He influenced the Rama Krishna-Vivekananda Movement of the nineteenth and twentieth centuries.

Knowledge is power. Power can be acquired either through knowledge or money or both. Here Saraswati and Laxmi come into picture, because the former is the goddess of knowledge and the latter is the goddess of wealth, the material prosperity. Can the Indian feminists dispense with knowledge or wealth to fight with a phallocentric world? One of the reasons as to why Indian women are incapable of fighting with this phallocentric world is illiteracy and it, in turn, is connected with poverty.

Much Indian feminist outbursts against traditional roles of mythological females, like Sita, Savitri, Draupadi and Damayanti, are based on their acceptance of the patriarchal and androcentric worlds, meekly. This is based on the logocentric studies of Indian epics by the Orientalists. It is also due to the *differance* of the *dispositif* of these epics by many Indian scholars—male and female. I take up for consideration Sita to explicate my thesis. Earlier, I wrote about the importance of oral tradition in the composition of Hindu scriptures. In this oral tradition, the possibility of interpolation, intertextuality, intersubjectivity, and digression, is immense and indisputable. I place Sita's claim to universality in the *Ramayana*, in which there are, at least, three different recensions, *viz.*, 'C,' the Bengali recension, and Western Indian,

Kashmiri, recension. "The only explanation for the great differences between the recensions is the fact that the text of the epic was for a long period only handed down by oral transmission. It is conceivable that the order of the verses became dislocated in the memory of the rhapsodists, that the wording must often have suffered considerable changes, and that the singers of different regions made different additions and extensions respectively."[14] Sita's name signifies "field furrow," she came forth out of the earth, and Mother Earth received her again. The *Rigveda* mentions her. The *Grihyasutras* have personified her in an extremely life-like manner—"lotus-crowned, radiant in every limb [...] black eyed," and so on. She is accounted the wife of Indra or Parjanya, the rain god. In Valmiki's *Ramayana* she is the wife of Rama. She is depicted as docile, submissive, and *pativarta* by almost all commentators. Thus, the character of Sita in Valmiki's *Ramayana* is a study of intertextuality, drawn from the *Rigveda*, the *Grihyasutras*, and the Indira-Brita myth of the *Rigveda*. Similarly, according to Mullick, intersubjectivity of "the Uttarakanda (the *Ramayana*) and the Narayan section of the *Mahabharata* clearly establish the fact that the base of the two Indian Epics is the same, and that the thesis proposed to be propounded by both is the same. One is thus driven to the examination of the substrata of both in order to fix the Uttarakanda as the base of the Epic of the *Ramayana*, and the *Bharat Samhita* of the *Mahabharata*."[15]

Valmiki shows Sita's marriage with Rama along with other three marriages arranged on the same dais same day and same time in a very simple way. His successors in the *Ramayana* tradition celebrate only the marriage of Rama and, thus, deviate from Valmiki.

According to Valmiki, Ahalya did not remain a stone and Rama did not set his foot on her to revive her from the curse. The sage Gautama simply said that she would remain invisible to the external world till she sees Rama. Similarly, Lakshmana did not draw any boundary line asking Sita not to cross it when he left her alone in Panchavati. This line which came to be known as *lakshmana rekha* never existed in Valmiki. It is a very popular and indelible interpolation in the later versions of the epic.

My purpose in writing about interpolation, intertextuality, intersubjectivity, deviation, in Valmiki's *Ramayana* and its later versions, say, in Kirittibas of Bengal and Tulsidas of UP, is to situate Sita in the right feminine perspective, following the Indian mythology. Now, I would study the *Ramayana* and Sita from the anthropological point of view. Mr K.S. Singh culls the character of Sita from the popular culture, popular literature, of tribals. Singh foregrounds them in the *epoche* of meaning on Sita and the *Ramayana,* in which Sita assumes an unconventional literary norm. To begin with, some Munda scholars have written that Ayodhya was a village, Sita a tribal girl, born and found in a drought year, and Janaka no more than a peasant. Sita is whisked away by Ravana when she is grazing goats. There is a point of similarity here with the Karbi *Ramayana, Sabin Alun,* mentioned by Birendranath Datta.[16] The Bhils, acculturated tribal group, have the Bhilodi *Ramayana.* The Dublas have their own versions. For example, they have an account of Lakshmana which is different from the ideal younger brother portrayed in the classic *Ramayana.* There is another version among other tribes that speaks of Lakshmana's "relationship" with Sita.

On the origins of *manavas, vanaras* and *rakshasas,* there are interesting parallels in the descriptions given in Valmiki's *Ramayana* and modern ethnographic accounts. Two Indian anthropologists, G. Ramdas in his article "The Aboriginal Tribes in the *Ramayana* (1925)" and Makhanlal Roychoudhury in "The Tribal Life and Society Gathered from *Ramayana* (*Indian Folklore,* April-June, 1957)" mention that there were not much of a difference between *rakshasas* and *manavas* (to which Rama belonged). There was a mere difference of degree between the two social groups. For example, intoxicants were as much part of food and ritual for the *manavas* as for the *rakshasas.* Even Rama is mentioned as offering intoxicants to Sita. Drinks were offered by Rama and Sita to Bharata and his army when they arrived in Chitrakut in Uttar Pradesh.

The feminist obsession with the one dimensional study of Sita, situating her only in Valmiki and Tulsidas, is as fallacious as *New York Times*' characterization of Salman Rushdie's *Midnight Children* as "a Continent finding its voice" or Fredric

Jameson's lumping together of all third World Literature as necessarily national allegories.

The concept of "new woman" was to emerge later in the narratology of Indian male and female writers. Anand in *Gauri*, Rao in *The Serpent and the Rope*, Ismat Chugtai and Rasheed Jahan (in Urdu), M.K. Indira (in Kannada), Amrita Pritam, Shivani (in Hindi), and Kamala Das (in Malayalam) are some prominent writers. The list is not exhaustive. In Indo-English literature, Nayantara Sahgal, Anita Desai, Shashi Deshpande, are three prominent movelists, who have raised the question of marginality of Indian women in patriarchal structrue of Hindu society. But, their problematization of women's marginality mediated "their beliefs through the allowable forms of dominant structure."[17] No Indian writer—male or female—this far, has made the paradigm shift of the narration of the patriarchal claustrophobia to *pornoglossia*. This has led psychoanalyst, Sudhir Kakar, to write that in spite of modernization, urbanization, and education, a "formidable consensus on the ideal of womanhood [...] still (in the mid 1970s) governs the inner imagery of individual men and women as well as the social relations between them in both the traditional and modern sectors of the Indian community."[18]

To explicate the interpellation of the marginality of women, their resistance against patriarchal power, and their justified claim for power *jouissance*, and *genderlect*, I turn to the study of some women characters in Desai, Sahgal, Das, Deshpande, Namjoshi. Monisha, in Desai's *Voices in the City*, can be regarded "as a victim of Hindu familial ideology and patriarchal oppression. Her unfulfilled sexuality, her metaphorically and literally barren marriage, her lack of privacy, her waiting upon men, her material dependence despite her education, and her violent death are all marks of sexual colonization."[19] I quote a passage from the novel to situate her in the above-mentioned predicament:

> The Bow Bazar house [...] the reception arranged by the heads of this many-headed family. In the small of my back, I feel a surreptitious push from Jiban and am propelled forward into the embrace of his mother who [...] while placing her hand on my head in blessing,

> also pushes a little harder than I think is necessary, and still harder, till I realize what it means, and go down on my knees to touch her feet [...]. Another pair of feet appears to receive my touch, then another [...] More—I lose count—but many more. Feet before faces here [...] into the courtyard we go, in a procession, and the tiered balconies [...] rise all around us, shutting out light and enclosing shadows like stagnant well water. The balconies have metal railings [...]. Through the thick iron bars I lookout on other walls, other windows—other bars.[20]

This passage, which forms a part of Monisha's diary, has four tropes, *viz.* touching of feet, the dark balconies, confining metal railings, and impregnable iron bars. The trope of touching feet, of elderly, senior, respectable persons—male and female—is embedded in Hindu culture, just like kissing in Christian culture.

The second trope of the dark balconies can be the darkness of Indian women at large or an indication of women's latent sexuality and strength. Or, it can be of Calcutta's streets lined with "dark, gap-toothed houses where the half-dead and the half-alive live."[21]

The tropes of confining metal railings and impregnable iron bars are called enclosure and incarceration by almost all women writers/activists. In Hindu family structure, the family is the site for disciplinary exercise. Discipline sometimes require enclosure. The family lies at the heart of society:

> Between family, society, and religious institutions, the family influences man's life most deeply and profoundly. Hence, for the preservation and development of life, the family should be considered as more important than society and religious institutions, and primary attention should be given to the development and enrichment of the family.[22]

Nirad C. Chaudhuri writes about a middle-class house in Calcutta:

> The middle-class house was small, sometimes even as small as twenty-five feet square [...]. There was also an impression of bareness, for these households possessed

> only a minimum of furniture [...] the rear was brought up by immense piles of bedding and rolls of mats and a vast assortment of earthen pots and pitchers, empty tins of all sizes and shapes, bottles and jars, and sacks for the storeroom, and iron, brass, and earthen pots and pans for the kitchen.[23]

The main purpose in erecting iron bars and metal railings in Calcutta is to turn its surrounding space for keeping rejects and items mentioned by Chaudhuri. The tropes of iron bars and metal railings are, therefore, not for incarceration for Monisha. Anita Desai, obsessed with her crusade for emancipation of women, has adopted displacement of the whole issue of gender. On the other hand, Rama Mehta, in her novel *Inside the Haveli*, has charted a teleological path for Hindu women. Why did Monisha choose madness and death and Geeta life in *Inside the Haveli* is answered by Rama Mehta herself in her sociological study:

> It was clear from the response (of the women interviewed) that Western attitudes and values in the domestic realm are not respected, nor is the Western concept of individualism felt to be worth emulating [...]. It shows that developing countries in the process of modernization want to maintain their way of life and want change but on the foundations of their cultural values.[24]

Richard Lannoy, a Western scholar, writes:

> In this century (20th) Indian women [...] have proved themselves more equal to their, as yet, only partially accomplished emancipation, and have not lost their essential feminity. Even when they become highly competent in professional life Indian women show no sign of acquiring those masculine traits of behaviour which are familiar in their counterparts in Anglo-Saxon countries. Their sense of power is already sufficiently deeply rooted in, and identified with, the family [...] for them to feel no need to resort to the kinds of aggressive assertion which intensely competitive, male-dominated Western societies demand.[26]

Anita Desai had written *Voices in the City* in 1965 and her foreclosure of feminine exclosure in social forestry in the post-Nehruvian period is non-teleological, a *satellite event* that *gatekeeps* fresh waves of *syllepses of events*.

Nayantara Sahgal's Sonali in *Rich Like Us* is a career woman, has a Woolfian "room of her own." She represents that "good" India and also modern Indian womanhood. She is an IAS, finds Gandhian precepts more attractive and acceptable than "straight and narrow doctrine" of Marxism. Unlike her childhood friend Ravi Kachra, who is also an IAS, she does not toe fashionable and practical party lines. When she was at Oxford, she questioned the influence of a heavy dose of Westernization on the Indian mind. She put it thus:

> But I couldn't understand why we had to keep cutting and pasting Western concepts together and tying ourselves to them for ever as if Europe were the centre of the universe, and the *Bible* and Marx were the last word on mankind.[26]

Anita Desai's reliance on Western concepts and Gayatri Chakravorty Spivak's reliance on Marxism, are examples of *passe* in Sahgal. The latter's *sociolect* is truly Indian. The narrative in *Rich Like Us*, through *internal focalization*, focuses through the consciousness of Sonali and Nishi; the narrative in *Voices in the City*, through *external focalization*, focuses on Monisha. I would quote two passages to explicate *internal focalization* in Sonali and Nishi. Sonali, during her illness, does some hard thinking and asks a question:

> What if there was a collective will to cowardice, when men and women in their millions, a whole nationful, did cowardly deeds? Was there a way out of that ?[27]

Nishi has given birth to a child. She likes to focus on the marginalized state of her mind during childbirth:

> Her selves lay torn in jagged halves on the delivery table, under the masked indifferent scrutiny of strangers and their implements, [...] her cry deranging no one but herself [...]. A stranger laid the child she hadn't wanted [...]. Through slitted battlements, [...] she could smile [...]. Grappling with her selves was simple if she kept her inner and outer selves apart.[28]

Sonali, unlike Monisha, is imagining herself neither in the likeness of Kali "building the funeral pyres of her own children,"[29] nor sharing her "dark way of thinking and feeling through life towards death."[30] Sonali, like Rose, speaks the language of love in a world in which lupine hunger for money and power is irrepressible. Viney Kirpal's critique of Sonali is pertinent: The portrait of Sonali is a progressive one; it spells hope for the upliftment of and emancipation of Indian women through education, economic freedom and self-determination. Like other feminist writers, Sahgal has not addressed herself solely to anti-male issues. Like them, she seeks the transformation and reformation of Indian society and through that, the freedom for the woman.[31]

Sahgal's admiration for Rose as Sita of the *Ramayana* is a trope for timeless quality of human actions and memory, "No good or evil deed, nothing great or small, was ever wiped out [...]."[32]

Nishi's *internal focalization*, mentioned above, finds echo in Saru's sex *jouissance* with her husband on the wedding night. "The intimate feelings and emotions of the women characters are caught in fine detail as if viewed under high-powered microscope."[33]

Terrorism is a term coined by the French writer Jean Paulhan and made use of by Gerard Genette. It is also "used more pejoratively to suggest a method of argumentation that is unprincipled and aggressive (and often sexist)."[34] Virginia Woolf says: "a woman is saying what she feels (as Joyce does)," and that is, she is writing without censoring, like a modernist, about everything her mind and body are experiencing. Such writing is *terrorism* and Saru's *internal focalization* of sex *jouissance* exemplifies Woolfian thesis. On the other hand, Nishi's intimate, secret feeling "increases the sensitivity of others towards a woman's world of feelings, emotions, even insecurities related to her biology."[35] The former follows the *camp* writing while the latter open-minded writing.

The fear of darkness in Shashi Deshpande's *The Dark Holds No Terrors* is not because of androcentric and patriarchal society, but of *meconnaissance,* derived from her ideological blindness to reality. Saru's careerist persona and domestic life are decentred. There is always a slippage between tergiversation, pride, egoism and horror, uncertainty, surrender to tradition, in her life.

Shashi Deshpande's Saru is unthroned by Kamala Das's Manasi from the realm of modern-day Indian feminism. Apart from the writing of Khushwant Singh, Chaman Nahal, and Upamanyu Chatterjee, which is *paraliterature*, no male Indian writer, like Lawrence, Claudel, Breton, Stendhal, Norman Mailer, and Henry Mailer, has portrayed women as adjuncts to the central quest of men heroes for selfhood. There is neither the language of *pornoglossia* nor of *phallocentrism*, in any male writing in Indo-English literature. Simone de Beauvoir's *The Second Sex* (1951) and Kate Millet's *Sexual Politics* (1970) were born to lead against male chauvinism of writers, mentioned above.

Kamala Das's *Alphabet of Lust* inaugurates an arguable undeveloped Laodicean woman character, Manasi, who "rents out" her body to Vijay Raje for a pair of diamond earrings and, second, repackaging herself, for political *jouissance*, to the Prime Minister. Her adulterous liaison with Raje nets her a *Padamshri*, India's highest literary-cultural award, and enables her to run for electoral office in Bengal. Her rentable body and political ambitions bring her closer to the Prime Minister who, in turn, repays her with the posts of Minister of Information and Broadcasting, then Home Minister, and finally the Prime Minister. Shirley Lim lauds Manasi, for her "only corruption is in the area of the sexual"[36] she also lauds Manasi's aggressive sexuality—"let me hunt in my own way," she says[37]—for dismantling orthodox gender hierarchies. Das, following Woolfian thesis, deconstructs the national-sexual text inscribed on the body of Manasi as (political) prostitute.

Suniti Namjoshi overdoes the problematic of Indian feminism by an overdose of female sexuality, that is, by linking herself with the lesbian, feminist, diasporic Indian's search for a country, in the 1986 collection *Flesh and Paper*, which she co-authored with her lover Gillian Hanscombe. But, I am here concerned with her novel *The Mothers of Maya Diip* (1989). Jyanvi is an Indian lesbian feminist poet in a fabulous island, in which "matriarchy bloom(s) unashamedly," blessed by "the goddess" and ruled by "a happy line of competent queens,"[38] the island ostensibly flourishes under the "just, gentle and generous"[39] Rule of the Mothers. Maya Diip, at least in conception, is Ladyland of Rokeya Hossain, discussed above. But, its execution is different from that of Ladyland. In Rokeya's story of Ladyland, the "asymmetrical men-women relations that are so obviously privileged towards men have been deconstructed, quite unconsciously at times."[40] Namjoshi "deconstructs nationalist idealization of India as nurturing mother in *The Mothers of Maya Diip,* but she offsets the male desexualizing of woman into a maternal automaton, androgynous virgin, or unsexed goddess and undercuts the hegemonic erotic ethos and normative Hindu male construction of feminity-in-nationalism by celebrating Jyanvi's lesbian sexual desire for Saraswati, thereby also writing the story of lesbianism into the discourse of nation-formation [...]. Namjoshi mounts a radical, sexualized challenge to the centuries—long silencing of lesbianism in Indian religious and secular (national) discourse."[41] Mann, implicitly, indicts Namjoshi as "the diasporic feminist who returns periodically to the native country, bringing with her knowledge of imported theories and ideologies; [...]."[42] Lesbian studies emerged in Western hemisphere in the 1980s as a kind of annexe of feminist criticism, before acquiring disciplinary independence. Namjoshi's diasporic search for a country leads her to an imagined country, Maya Diip, far away from India that we all know, recognize, and accept.

Shashi Deshpande or Nayantara Sahgal or Kamala Das, unlike Anita Desai and Suniti Namjoshi, is "the indigenous, decolonized/ing intellectual, who ostensibly speaks with an authentic voice but whose position is compromised by its generally elitist, urban locus."[43]

The construction of women as 'Other' in First-world and Third-world, feminism, is a misnomer. I particularly refer to Gayatri Chakravorty Spivak, a diasporic feminist, who says that "Women are universally oppressed by men." Her hypothesis stems from her deep study of a connivance between Hindu patriarchy and British imperialism. Her essay "Can the Subaltern Speak?," is derived from studying the discourse of *sati,* in which the Hindu patriarchal code converged with colonialism's narrativization of Indian culture to efface all traces of woman's voice. Benita Parry counters this hypothesis of Spivak:

> From the discourse of *Sati* Spivak derives large, general arguments on woman's subject constitution/object formation in which the subaltern woman is conceived as a homogeneous and coherent category [...]. Since the native woman is constructed within multiple social relationships and positioned as the product of different class, caste and cultural specificities, it should be possible to locate traces and testimony of women's voice on those sites where women inscribed themselves as healers, ascetics, singers of sacred song, artisans and artists, and by this to modify Spivak's model of the silent subaltern.[44]

Anne Maxwell opposes the decentring of *telos* of Spivakian feminism by Benita Parry and accuses her of being "fairly and squarely within First World feminist discourse" which "attempts to articulate a separate women's identity for western and non-western women alike through the recovery of a separate female tradition [...]."[45]

Benita Parry's concept of feminism is suitable for Indian space, which is multilayered, multicoloured, multicultural, multilingual and which demands multiple lives, not *contiguous* lives. Is it possible to box in Desai, Deshpande, Das, Namjoshi and Sahgal with Mahasweta Devi (Bengali), Gauri Deshpande and Chhaya Datar (Marathi), in the genre of fiction? Is it possible to box in Toru Dutt and Sarojini Naidu with Amrita Pritam (Hindi) and Indira Sant (Marathi), in the genre of poetry? Is it possible to box in Santha Rama Rau with Gail Omvedt, in the genre of prose? Using Louis Althusser's title of his essay, I find "Contradiction and Overdetermination" in Indian feminism.

NOTES

1. Partha Chatterjee, "Colonialism, Nationalism and Colonised Women: The Contest in India," *American Ethnologist*, Vol. 16, No. 4, 622.
2. Himani Bannerji, "Projects of Hegemony: Towards a critique of Subaltern Studies 'Resolution of the Women's Question,'" Mumbai: *Economic and Political Weekly*, Vol. XXXV, No. 11, March 11-17, 2000, 911.
3. Quoted in Geoffrey Moorhouse's *India Britannica*, London: Harvill Press, 1983, 124.

4. Arun P. Mukherjee, "The Exclusions of Postcolonial Theory and Mulk Raj Anand's *Untouchable*: A Case Study," *Ariel*, Vol. 23, No. 3, July 1991, 32.
5. Hansa Mehta, *Indian Woman*, Delhi: Butala & Company, 1981, 186.
6. J. Murdoch (Comp.), *Twelve Years of Indian Progress, Extracted From the Indian National Congress*; The resolutions of its Thirteen Sessions, Madras, 1898, 36.
7. Syed Manzoorul Islam, "Subaltern's World View: A Reading of *Sultana's Dream*," in *Infinite Variety: Women in Society and Literature*, eds. Firdous Azim and Niaz Zaman, Dhaka: University Press, 1994, 116.
8. Gayatri Chakravorty Spivak, "Can the Subaltern Speak?" in *The Post-Colonial Studies Reader*, eds. Bill Ashcroft, Gareth Griffith, Helen Tiffin, London and New York: Routledge, 1995, 28.
9. Quoted in *Political Mythology and Popular Fiction*, eds. Ernest J. Yanarella and Lee Sigelman, Westport, Conn: Greenwood, 1988, 7.
10. Edward Said, *Orientalism: Western Conceptions of the Orient*, 3rd edn. Harmondsworth: Penguin, 1992 (1978), 3.
11. Richard Fox, "East of Said," *Edward Said: A Critical Reader*, ed. Michael Sprinker, Oxford: Blackwell, 1992, 151.
12. Leela Gandhi, *Postcolonial Theory*, Delhi: OUP, 1999 (1998), 78.
13. Tejaswini Niranjana, *Siting Translation*, Hyderabad: Orient Longman Ltd., 1995 (1992), 20.
14. M. Winternitz, *A History of Indian Literature*, Calcutta: University of Calcutta, Vol. 1, Part II, 1978 (3rd edition), 438.
15. Promatha Nath Mullick, *The Mahabharata As It was and Shall Be: A Critical Study*, Allahabad: The Pioneer Press, 1934, 172.
16. Birendranath Datta, "*Sabin Alun*: The Karbi *Ramayana*," in *The Journal of the Assam Research Society*, Guwahati, Vol. 27, 1983.
17. Elaine Showalter, "Feminist Criticism in the Wilderness," in *The New Feminist Criticism: Essays on Women, Literature and Theory*, ed. Elaine Showalter, London: Virago, 1986, 261.
18. Sudhir Kakar, *Inner World*, Delhi: OUP, 1989 (1978), 68.
19. Harveen Sachdeva Mann, 'Going in the Opposite Direction': Feminine Recusancy in Anita Desai's *Voices in the City*,' *Ariel*, Vol. 23, No. 4, Oct. 1992, 85.
20. Anita Desai, *Voices in the City*, Delhi: Orient, 1988 (1965), 109.
21. *Ibid.*, p. 92.
22. Satischandra Chakrabarti, *Nabayuger ahvan*, quoted in *Texts of Power: Emerging Disciplines in Colonial Bengal*, ed. Partha Chatterjee, Calcutta: Samya, 1996 (1995), p. 128.
23. Nirad C. Chaudhuri, *The Autobiography of an Unknown Indian*, Bombay: Jaico, 1969 (1951), 388.

24. Rama Mehta, *The Western Educated Hindu Woman*, Mumbai: Asia, 1970, 207.
25. Richard Lannoy, *The Speaking Tree: A Study of Indian Culture and Society*, London: OUP, 1971, 130-31.
26. Nayantara Sahgal, *Rich Like Us* (1983), London: Sceptre Edition, 1987, 113.
27. *Ibid.*, 35.
28. *Ibid.*, 234.
29. Anita Desai, *Voice in the City*, 237.
30. *Ibid.*, 175.
31. Viney Kirpal, "*Rich Like Us*: Text, Context and Subtext" in *Women's Writing: Text and Context*, ed. Jasbir Jain, Jaipur: Rawat Publication, 1996, 177.
32. Nayantara Sahgal, *Rich Like Us*, 115.
33. Viney Kirpal, 171.
34. Jeremy Hawthorn, *A Concise Dictionary of Contemporary Literary Theory*, London: Edward Arnold, 1992, p. 188.
35. Viney Kirpal, 172.
36. Shirley Geok-Lin Lim, "Semiotics, Experience and the Material Self: An Inquiry into the Subject of the Contemporary Asian Writer," *Women's Studies*, Vol. 18, 1990, 159.
37. Kamala Das, *Alphabet of Lust*, Delhi: Orient Paperbacks, 1976, 46.
38. Suniti Namjoshi, *The Mothers of Maya Diip*, London: Women's Press, 1989, 5.
39. *Ibid.*, 14.
40. Syed Manzoorul Islam, 116.
41. Harveen Sachdeva Mann, " Cracking India": Minority Women Writers and the Contentious Margins of Indian Nationalist Discourse," *Journal of Commonwealth Literature*, Vol. XXIX, No. 2, 1994, 86.
42. Harveen Sachdeva Mann, "Women's Rights versus Feminism?: Postcolonial Perspectives," 77.
43. *Ibid.*, 77.
44. Benita Parry, "Problems in Current Theories of Colonial Discourse," *The Post-Colonial Studies Reader*, 37.
45. Anne Maxwell, " The Debate on Current Theories of Colonial Discourse," *Kunapipi*, Vol. XIII, No. 3, 1991, 80.

15

FEMINISM TODAY: A PERSPECTIVE

T.M.J. INDRA MOHAN

During the last century, the feminist writing has cut across multiple and contradictory traditions presenting the most fundamental challenges in terms of its relevant subjectivity and the category of experience. Simone de Beauvoir's *The Second Sex* (1948) had initiated the process of analysing the social constructions of gender and of distinguishing between sex and gender. Kate Milletts *Sexual Politics* (1970) analysed the sex role and the oppression of women under patriarchal social organisation. Particularly in America, in the 1970's, women thinker concentrated on analyzing the 'images' of women represented in or constructed through cultural forums such as literature, as well as on the economic position of women as a consequence of the division of labour and the organisation of the family. By the mid 1970's there was increased attention from both broadly socialist or radical feminists who voiced through texts their views championing women's cause.

Feminist schools of thought can be divided into two distinct varieties. The first type is concerned with woman as reader. Woman as the consumer of male produced literature and the second is concerned with woman as writer who produces textual meaning with the history, themes, genres and structures of literature. Their work become essentially political and polemical with theoretical applications of sociology and aesthetics in a self-contained and experimental way. Gynocritics, research relating to feminist research in history, anthropology, psychology and sociology, all have developed hypotheses about a female subculture, the internalised constructs of feminity, and also the occupations, interactions, and consciousness of women. Anthropologists studied the female subculture in the relationships between women, as mothers, daughters, sisters and friends.

Feminism should attempt in seeing itself as a component of Enlightened modernism in which meaningful relationship needs to be built up between male and female in terms of socio-cultural amity. It need not become a socio-political force which in turn will thwart an objective evaluation of feminist ideals and writings. We should rather consider feminism as a movement for social change. The post 1968 saw the emergence of a new political group demanding for legal and financial equality. Firestone's *The Dialectic of Sex* (1970) a text of revolution who insisted that the work be called the 'pioneer western feminist movement.' Millett's *Sexual Politics* (1970) and Firestone's *The Dialectic of Sex* (1970) sought to reclaim a feminist history and they identified feminism as theoretical standpoint with the women's movement as political practice.

Annette Kuhn's *The Power of Image* (1985) shows that feminism has regarded ideas, language and image as crucial in shaping women's lives. Feminism has been taken as an object of both analysis and intervention in the construction of knowledge, meaning and representations. It has also been concerned with the struggle to find a voice through which such knowledge might be expressed. According to Rosalind Delmar feminism has sought to transform economic position from that of object of knowledge to knowing subject, from the state of subjections to subjecthood (in J. Mitchell and A. Gkaley, eds. *What is Feminism* (1986). Feminism's initial project ties theoretical oppression to a narrative emancipation through social transformation. In 1970's emerged a new feminist concern from the practical domain of an emergent feminist politics. In this wave of feminism, difference came to signify all the theoretical complexities arising from the sociological observation that women do not possess a uniform social identity. Postmodern thoughts and difference in feminism come together in a fragile form, in consequence both recognise the practical and epistemological significance of women being variously situated, like men in a network of many dimensions of identity and power.

Donna Haraway has attempted in formulating a feminist approach to nature and techno-science. The work seeks to analyse the impact of technological development on both the feminism and society.

Haraway, as a feminist, is concerned with challenging the traditional postulation of nature as the site of origin and identity. She attempts to portray female subjectivity as contingent upon the influence of class, race and politics in consequence of which she becomes the product of society. The popular aspect of Haraway's thought is that what proffers notion of identity also transcends the polarities of the nature or technology opposition. To exist between such dualism, suspended between rejection and appropriation, is what Haraway defined as a 'Cyborg' subject position. Her essay "A Cyborg Manifesto" was published in 1985 but remains her best known piece of writing. For Haraway, the Cyborg, who is neither wholly natural nor artefactual, becomes the embodiment of the postmodern condition. Though it may be argued that the feminine is ignored and suppressed in the masculine order women should seize the first available opportunity to construct their own subjectivity on their own terms. If they attempt courageously it would abolish the distinction between centre and margins altogether.

The post feminist contention is that the dangers and damage of feminism 'prove' women are wrong to claim equality in the male-dominated world. Post feminism defends men and calls 'feminism' as the disease of social and economic evils.

Around 1970's, there was much momentum having been gained through text authored by liberal or socialist or radical feminists. This approach was formulated by Elaine Showalter as the basis of 'Gynocriticism' and her *A Literature of Their Own* (1971) attempted to construct an alternative way of presenting female writing and experience.

Anthropologists study the female subculture in the relationship between women, as mothers, daughters, sisters and friends.

In the symbolic social concepts, women are used as a basis for female solidarity and worth and they are the beings who with their social resources on which they build a society of their own. Ann Douglas's *The Feminization of Amercian Culture*, focuses the genesis of American mass culture in the sentimental literature of women. The bond of womanhood in women's literature is well highlighted by Nina Auerbach's *Communities of Women: An Idea in Fiction.*

The very idea of separate domain for women's writing began from the 1840's to 1880—when they wrote by masculine models but with female concerns. During the second stage till 1920s they formulated specific female protests and demands and in the third stage from 1920 to the present, women's writing with a commitment moves towards self-discovery and the exploration of an inner space of female experience. The strong wave in the 1970's and 1980's feminism concentrated on transforming the intellectual fields and playing a significant role in directing academic focus on the concerns of 'otherness' and marginalization. It turned towards female experience as the source of autonomous art, extending the ferminist analysis of culture to the forms and techniques of literature. Their experiments were both enriching and re-enervating. Much of their literature and criticism expanded and transferred the existing theoretical models. Simone de Beauvoir pointed out in her book *The Second Sex* (1949), that woman in western thought has represented the *other* that can confirm man's destiny as a rational thinking being. According to her the category of the *other* is primordial as consciousness itself, since the Self can only be defined in opposition to something which is not self. Man, he says, has assigned to himself the category of self, and constructed woman as *other*. Thereby he made himself as the subject, he became the absolute-She is the other. These are all the problems due to liberal interpretation of feminism and feminist literature and theory. As Sandra Harding in *Knowing Women* remarks that contemporary 'instabilities' of feminism's analytical categories will make feminist thought—cut off from the sources of feminism's transformative possibilities.

In the broadest possible sense, the contribution of women to literature could make a significant difference to the judgments and practices of the whole society. Over the ages in the male-dominated world, women are kept out of the cultural traditions which ultimately resulted in open rebellion by the women writers. When the opportune time came to revalue women's writing, men began to make a biased version of literary history and women's work came under bitter criticism. Despite changing socio-political scenario world over, justice to women's writing has not been done.

In the current academic and literary world, what we come across in is the catalogued achievements of males and they all help to suggest that women are without literary tradition and output. It ultimately leads to insinuations about female inferiority. It also erodes women's confidence and undermines the woman writer. It is now time to act and invent a literary tradition which should create a positive influence on women and women's literary endeavours.

Women's writing must transcend masculine models and feminist protests and demands and also the scenarios of compromise. It should also cease to be merely a propagandist literature seeking liberation movement and equal rights. It should create a purposeful awakening and reinvigorate mythologies of female culture in an appropriate genre. The preconceived concept of women as a symbol of sex needs to be redefined in terms of socio psychological framework.

On the ideological plane feminism raises fundamental questions about women's writing, reading and gender bias. It is an operating force behind the interdisciplinary tool for social and cultural analysis and as a political practice. Thus feminism has transformed the perceptions of life and literature. According to Bell Hooks, in the ultimate analysis feminism dismantles all systems of domination. In the rational analysis, "feminism emerges as a concept that can encompass both on ideology and movement for socio-political change based on a critical analysis of male privilege and women's subordination within any given society" (Offen 151). It is pro-woman but not anti-man. The whole idea of feminism revolves round only value based systems and recognition rather than need based and gender biased. It aims at overcoming male hierarchy in the most profound sense and ask for, in a simple language, a treatment as an individual human being. In consequence, feminist thought emerges as 'humanist' thought. Virginia Woolf herself advocates humanist thought in her *Three Guineas Three*

Causes first to prevent war by encouraging pacifist society, second building an institution for women, third, establishing a society in the cause of helping woman to enter the professions.

In a way all-round development centering the women, instead of marginalising, could bury the hatchet and pave way for a dynamic social order world over devoid of gender codes would help in building a new social order with a positivist and holistic approach to life which will in turn create only human and ethical values inherent in every individual irrespective of sex. Women live by truth which needs to be honoured.

REFERENCES

Abel, Elizabeth. *Race Class and Psychoanalysis.* Hirsch and Keller, 1990.

Addams, Jane. *Democracy and Social Ethics.* New York: MacMillan Co., 1902.

Armstrong, Isobel. *New Feminist Discourses, Critical Essays on Theories and Tenets.* London: Routledge, 1992.

Barrett, Michele. *Feminism and the Definition of Cultural Politics.* In Rosalind Brunt and Caroline Rowan, (eds.). *Feminism Culture and Politics.* London: Lawrence and Wishart Ltd., 1982.

Belsey, Catherine (eds.). *The Feminist Reader.* London: Macmillan, 1989.

Carden, Maren Lockwood. *The Feminist Movement.* New York: Russell Sage Foundation, 1974.

Eisentein, Hester. *Contemporary Feminist Thoughts.* London: Unwin Paperbacks, 1984.

Fuss, Diana. *Essentially Speaking Feminism, Nature and Difference.* New York: Routledge, 1989.

Firestone, Shulamith. *The Dialectic of Sex: The Case for Feminist Revolution.* New York: Bantam Books, 1970.

Millett, Kate. *Sexual Politics.* New York: Doubleday, 1970.

Offen, Karen. "Defining Feminism: A Comparative Historical Approach," *Signs* 14, 1 (Autumn 1988): 119-57.

Rice, Philip and Waugh Patricia. *Modern Literary Theory A Reader* 2nd edition. Edward Arnold. London, 1992.

Showalter, Elaine, (ed.). *The New Feminist Criticism, Essay on Women Literature and Theory.* New York: Pantheon Books, 1985.

Singh, Sushila. *Feminism: Theory, Criticism Analysis.* Delhi: Pencraft International, 1997.

Sim, Stuart. *The-Icon Critical Dictionary of Post-Modern Thought.*

'O, THOSE EXTRAORDINARY WOMEN!'

Often, indeed, I had occasion to remember that cynical remark of Swift—that, after all, as respects mere learning, the most accomplished woman is hardly on a level with a schoolboy [...]. I am well aware that they have their peculiar province. But that province does not extend to learning *technically so-called.*

—De Quincey

A woman's learning is like the fine clothes of an upstart who is anxious to exhibit all the world the riches so unexpectedly acquired.

—Elizabeth Smith (who had nine languages under her belt)

She tumbled early, by accident or design, into a spacious closet of good English reading. Had I twenty girls, they should be brought up exactly in this fashion. I know not whether their chance in wedlock might not be diminished by it; but I can answer for it that it makes (if the worst comes to the worst) most incomparable old maids.

—Charles Lamb about Mary Ann Lamb

Real business and real leisure make up the portions of men's time whereas women in the home have little real leisure, which may be reason some are so dull and unattractive to their husbands.

—Mary Ann Lamb

We had a vague impression that authoresses are liable to be looked on with prejudice.

—Charlotte Bronte

Literature cannot be the business of a woman's life and it ought not to be. The more she is engaged in her proper duties, the less leisure will she have for it, even as an accomplishment and a recreation.

—Robert Southey

The daydreams in which you habitually indulge are likely to induce a distempered state of mind and, in proportion as all the ordinary uses of the world seem to you flat and unprofitable, you will be unfitted for them without being fitted for anything else.

—Robert Southey to Charlotte Bronte

There is nothing I fear so much as idleness, the want of occupation [...] the lethargy of the faculties [...] I should not know this lethargy if I could write [...]. But that cannot be—it is not to he thought of [...].

—Charlotte Bronte

Another sign of the times is Female Authorship. These have been great, and are constantly increasing. Women have taken possession of so many provinces for which men had pronounced them unfit, that though these still declare there are some inaccessible to them, it is difficult to say just where *they might stop.*

—Margaret Fuller, 1845

Very early I knew that the only object in life was to grow.

—Margaret Fuller

It was greatly superior to all I knew before, in fact the undeniable utterances of a true historic mind. Altogether unique among the Writing Women of this generation. Rare enough too, God knows among the Writing Men.

—Carlyle on Margaret Fuller's Writing

Who would be a goodie if they could be a genius?

—Margaret Fuller

To see a lady of such taste,
So slatternly is shocking:
Your pen and poetry lay by
And learn to darn your stockings.

—Nineteenth-Century Popular Rhyme

America is wholly given over to a d—d mob of scribbling women [...] no chance of success while the public taste is occupied with their trash—and should be ashamed of myself if I did succeed.

—Nathaniel Hawthorne

I, the author of Uncle Tom's Cabin? *No, indeed! The Lord himself wrote it, and I was but the humblest instrument in His wise hand. To him alone be all the praise.*

—Harriet Beech Stowe

The Queen is most anxious to enlist everyone who can speak or write to join in checking this mad wicked folly of Women's Rights, with all its attendant horrors, on which her poor, feeble sex is bent, forgetting every sense of womanly feeling and propriety.

—Letter of Queen Victoria to Mrs Theodore Martin

CONTRIBUTORS

Partha Pratim Dasgupta. Senior Lecturer in English, Hooghly Mohsin College, Chinsurah, Hooghly, West Bengal.

T.M.J. Indra Mohan. Professor, Department of English, Pachaiyappa's College, Chennai, Tamil Nadu.

Anita Singh. Reader, Department of English, Vasanta College for Women, Rajghat, Varanasi, Uttar Pradesh.

Nandini Sahu. Department of English, IACR, Rayagada, Orissa.

Rama Kundu. Professor of English, Burdwan University, Burdwan, West Bengal.

Santwana Haldar. Reader, Department of English, F.M. Auto. College, Balasore, Orissa.

A.K. Awasthi. Professor of English, Dr Harisingh Gour University, Sagar, Madhya Pradesh.

Beulah Ranjitsingh. Reader, Sarah Tucker College, Tirunelveli, Tamil Nadu.

Ajay Kumar Ghosh. Assistant Teacher of English, Vill. Mosra. P.O. Somra, Dt. Hooghly, West Bengal.

Mohua Ghosh. Assistant Teacher of English, Balagarh Uccha Vidyalaya, Zeerut, Hooghly, West Bengal.

Jaydeep Sarangi. Lecturer in English, Bacchurdova, Jhargram, West Midnapore, West Bengal.

Smriti Singh. Ad hoc Lecturer, Department of English, Patna Women's College, Bihar.

Shyam S. Agarwalla. Principal, Dr Ram Manohar Lohia College, Ranchi University, Ranchi, Jharkhand.